Leading Quakers:
Disciple Leadership, A Friends Model

Jennifer L. Isbell

E A R L H A M
SCHOOL *of* RELIGION

Earlham Press
Richmond, Indiana

Leading Quakers: Disciple Leadership, A Friends Model

Library of Congress Cataloging-In-Publication Data

Isbell, Jennifer L, 1971
Leading Quakers: Disciple Leadership, A Friends Model/Jennifer L. Isbell
ISBN 978-1-879117-20-4

1. Religion   2.Quakerism

2008931275

DEDICATION

With gratitude and deep affection for the faithful example so apparent in the lives you live, I dedicate this book to three dear Friends: Paul, Michael, and Jay. May God's joy continue to unfold through you.

TABLE OF CONTENTS

What You Are Holding
in Your Hands

This is a book about the nuts and bolts of identifying the needs and gifts of your worshipping community. The source and guiding image for this book and for the model of leadership presented here is the Incarnation. Jesus is the love of God made manifest in the world. As we encounter the living Christ in worship and in the world, we are reminded of what it means that God incarnates. Our loving and faithful response is to work at incarnating ourselves—at living our lives responsively, faithfully, and ethically, bringing into full manifestation our own witness to the love of God. As Friends, we are deeply committed to the corporate experience of being called into community and called as community. In this way, we become Bodies of Christ in the world.

An issue currently facing the church, and the Religious Society of Friends, is defining the needs and vision for ministry in the 21st century. "Where does God call us to be, and how will we get there from here?" This book invites worshipping communities to sit together, in the sometimes uncomfortable presence of God and one another, with these very difficult and essential questions.

Welcome to the Beginning

It is ironic to be welcoming you to the beginning, when really the beginning will only begin when your work with this book is finished. From my childhood I remember being teased and provoked by the question of why when people enter the front of a church they are often automatically at the back of the worship room. Similarly, the front door approach offered by this book will lead you to a starting point from which you can move forward in your worship community.

While *Leading Quakers: Disciple Leadership, A Friends Model* is the end of an intense year of working to produce a concrete and unmistakably Quaker resource that addresses leadership and vitality concerns in the Religious Society of Friends, it is also the culmination of many years of deep listening and information-gathering by Earlham School of Religion. This resource is available because ESR is attentive to the needs of the Religious Society of Friends in the 21st century, and because many Friends across the theological spectrum have come together in conversations to be transparent and faithful, seeking to witness to one another and to the world about what Quakerism has to offer the larger Christian movement and all persons of faith.

My own part in the development of this resource has been an amazing occasion of Grace for which I am deeply grateful. I came to ESR hoping to "trade in" or "upgrade" the gifts I had discovered unfolding in myself. What happened instead was a compelling, theologically, historically, scripturally and experientially sound journey through the most intense spiritual reflection on the most personal material I could imagine. If I have become a new creature, it has been by learning the names of the seeds already planted in me, and by (mostly) willingly embracing the process of transformation. This is how I have come to understand spiritual formation, which is proof of God's continuing presence among us. This book is an offering for the spiritual formation of communities and the leaders that rise out of communities. I hope it can be of use, under the unending care of God, whose Love is a constant companion.

Ultimately our testimonies in the world are the way those who witness our lives come to know our faith and the God our faithful lives point to. May your ministry and the life of your meeting flourish in well-lived lives that are unmistakable in their source and their purpose!

A Plan for Unpacking

This book is divided into nine chapters and contains several resources in the appendices. Because of the culture-shifting potential of the information conveyed, and the individual and community self-awareness it encourages, the book is best used as a complete resource and followed in the order presented. In the next section, called "How to Use This Book," some suggestions are made for figuring out how best to implement a plan of study for your group, including ways to modify the materials. Here is a brief overview of what each chapter offers:

Chapter One lays the first brick in the foundation of common ground for meetings undertaking this study. It examines the vocabulary of faith used in the congregation by offering exercises for discussion of some terms that may be helpful to understanding the tools and gifts that are essential to discipleship, including authority, stewardship, obedience, and giftedness. In addition, readers are encouraged to bring these concepts out of the realm of personal opinion and into the realm of community understanding by looking at the monthly and yearly meeting practices of naming and nurturing gifts.

Chapter Two looks at the Biblical tradition of being called by God and invites readers to work on finding God in the verbs. You will be invited to reflect on your own moments of divine encounter, as individuals and in worshiping groups, and to begin to consciously note how God interacts with the world in your experience. Also in this chapter, readers will begin to explore the ways in which callings and leadings rise individually as well as out of a stated need in one's community.

Chapter Three invites readers to consider the ways in which their lives are their witness to the presence of God, noting that discipleship specifically indicates a way of relating to the Teacher, who in Quaker understanding is persistently available as Christ. Participants are invited to consider how callings, leadings, and concerns are regarded in their communities.

Chapter Four encourages participants to explore how their own worship community understands itself in relation to the understanding of the Body of Christ as Paul so often writes in his letters to early Church communities. Friends are invited to consider what membership means in their community practice and to name the ways in which leadership and volunteer roles are currently filled in the meeting.

Chapter Five is a Quaker model of what is commonly known as an "inventory of gifts" in other denominations. In the provided inventory, however, the same attention given to discerning one's own gifts is turned toward discerning the gifts of the meeting. By prayerfully examining these gifts side by side, readers may come to see themselves specifically called to the community and its purposes.

Chapter Six sets the stage for understanding why a Quaker model of leadership is a particular thing other than the popular model of Christian servant leadership. Because Friends worship in the spirit of expectancy, they are more suited and more inclined to a model of leadership that is based on discipleship. The Truth Friends serve is the glimpse each is afforded by one's encounter with God. Aligning one's life in response to both the faithful expectation of God's Presence and to the compelling desire to convert one's life to be responsive to that Presence *is* discipleship.

Chapter Seven picks up on the explanation of Disciple Leadership, tying together previous insights on the Body of Christ, the Incarnation, and the Presence of Christ. Readers are invited to add to a list of characteristics that describe the disciple leader and to concentrate on the relational nature of God and communities of faith.

Chapter Eight explores the image of the worshipping community as spiritual community and anchor. By considering meeting for worship and meeting for business, readers are asked to consider the ways in which they prepare for and participate in these practices and the ways in which they are willing to be changed by their participation in the community of faith.

Chapter Nine provides an outline for a meeting retreat, which can be done in a full day. The purpose of the material is to help individuals and the meeting reflect theologically on the group's identity and purpose. There are exercises for exploring elements of spiritual and social community already present in the group, and exercises for deepening the personal knowledge participants have of one another. By the end of the day and at the end of this book-length study, participants will have had opportunities to recommit to the corporate life of the meeting and to their individual worship lives. The questions one could be ready to answer include: *What is God calling this group to in this time? Who are the leaders and the leaders-to-be, and how can they be nurtured in their work? How can others follow with their gifts?*

How to Use This Book

During the year this book came together, a group of meetings from Western and Indiana Yearly Meetings volunteered to be the first participants in an ESR-sponsored leadership development program. From the feedback loops set in place during that year, suggestions came about how to make the most of this program in your local congregation.

1. Consider using the topics in this book as a program for a full year of study. Although there are nine chapters, the exercises and after-effects of each unit could easily carry an engaged group for a month of study or more.

2. Have the leadership facilitation team of four to six members complete the nine units of study before trying to lead it. Familiarity with the material and a sense of the foundation laid by following this study in the order in which it is presented, will increase the confidence and the preparedness of the facilitating team.

3. Consider having the meeting or church adopt a covenant of participation. This curriculum intends to be culture changing and will be most useful if it is granted a high level of commitment and participation. A sample covenant agreement is included in Appendix A.

4. Let the discernment process that leads up to participation be the foundation for getting commitments to participate. Use the queries in Appendix C for pastoral leadership, the meeting as a whole and for individuals who may be called to lead this study. Confirming an enthusiastic "Yes!" is an important first step to accepting the challenge of this study. If any of the three groups queried cannot commit to participate, prayerfully consider what obstacles can or may be lifted before proceeding.

5. Plan the year of study, including the discernment process, the facilitating group "speed study" of the materials, and planned times for reviewing progress to date. Checking in with participants outside of the Sunday school or other study forum will allow objective modification of the yearlong plan. Be open to revision. See Appendix B for a suggested plan for the year of study.

Friends, blessings of courage and the willingness to be transformed by the presence of God with you, as you undertake this work of exploring disciple leadership in the manner of Friends!

CHAPTER ONE

The Vocabulary of Faith and Giftedness

Early Friends, particularly Society founder George Fox, were convinced of an inward spiritual reality, which mirrored many of the main points in the life of Jesus. Like those the apostle Paul encourages with his letters, Friends are to be crucified in Christ that they may die and be born again in Christ. The experience of the inward Presence was both the encouragement and the goal of the worshipper's life, but as you may imagine, with the life of Jesus as a source for knowing those major spiritual events, the inward Presence is not always soothing or easy.

In his recent book, *On Living with a Concern for Gospel Ministry*,[1] New England minister Brain Drayton offers advice to Friends feeling called to ministry. Two important points he makes relate to the conditions in which modern gospel ministers are perceiving their leadings. In terms of context, he notes that the Biblical literacy and confidence in this literacy that were prominent in earlier times are not the norm today. Often the experience of Christ's invitation to move deeper into ministry is felt inwardly and results in the individual's pursuit of knowledge and improved spiritual practices as he or she feels encouraged to gain skills to assist in the work he or she feels called to. One may move toward

---

[1] Brian Drayton, *On Living With A Concern For Gospel Ministry* (Philadelphia: Quaker Press of Friends General Conference), 2005.

using new gifts before they are ripe, and if the contexts of such first flights are not themselves seasoned and appreciative of the sometimes slight movements of the Spirit, the minister in formation may falter unnecessarily. When apprehending a call, Drayton notes that one may be called to change the priorities of one's life, radically. He writes:

> It may be though, that God will sometimes (or increasingly) make it your duty to work harder than you are inclined to, make choices that will be hard or surprising, push you in ways that test your emotional, spiritual, or physical strength. If you are really under orders, and not merely moving according to your own designs, and desires, then you may well be taken off guard.[2]

He is writing with encouragement to those who might be feeling led to ministry. Take note, however, of the cautions he offers and what they indicate about the lives of those experiencing a call. God may make things harder, and it may come as a surprise. What is the role of a community that seeks to support Friends who may be in this confusing and challenging time of discernment?

It is important for meetings and churches to have awareness of the increases of gifts happening in their midst. Cultivating this kind of awareness is not unlike cultivating attention to one's own spiritual life or the spiritual life of the meeting. Drayton speaks of his and others' path in gospel ministry as including an "apprenticeship in the school of Christ." In this school, Scripture, experience, spiritual disciplines and

---

[2] Ibid., 37.

community are all places of encounter and increased wisdom. For these influences of the School of Christ to be known and gathered into the discernment and ministry development process, they must be read against the larger backdrop of our faith. For this work, we need a vocabulary that is deep and reflects meanings that are consistent with Friends' understandings.

Terms of Faith

Obedience	Discipleship	Authority
Worship	Stewardship	Gifts/Giftedness

This first chapter offers the chance to look at the vocabulary of our faith and to consider together the meanings we share and the sources from which we derive our understanding. Following are some definitions for you to consider. Edit and/or add to the definitions to make them match your understanding.

Obedience may be seen as a kind of collaboration with God.[3] For Friends, who understand there to be a seed of God in everyone, the collaboration is a responsive, progressive, committed relationship with Christ who is teacher, guide, and encourager.

---

[3] Brian Drayton uses the term *collaboration* this way in his book, cited above.

Discipleship is a kind of student-teacher relationship in which the student is not learning through academic inquiry alone, but through being present with the teacher and applying what is learned to one's life. Discipleship conveys an on-going relationship of learning and doing in a way that mirrors and responds to the teachings and to the teacher.

_____

_____

_____

Authority may be viewed in terms of (1) a way of being or teaching that is respected or conveys power, or (2) in classifying how a group or individual regards a source. By the first definition, we may refer to passages in Scripture, which indicate how Jesus was known to be truly anointed, because he taught as one with authority. In the second definition, we may think about our own hierarchy of sources of authority. In theology, there is the example of John Wesley's quadrilateral of religious authority. Various denominations place importance on one or more of the following. How would you rank them?

- Scripture (authoritative text, the Bible)
- Experience (personal or group experience)
- Reason (logic; thought)
- Tradition (what has come before the present time in Christianity or the Society of Friends)

_____

_____

_____

Worship among Friends is a time set aside to be gathered in community, expectantly waiting on God's message to/for those gathered. Preparation for being in this corporate state may involve varying combinations of hymn singing, a prepared message, reading Scripture as community, vocal ministry from the gathered body, and silence. Worship is the center of Friends churches and meetings. As persons in ministry move outward to serve from their private spiritual disciplines, meetings move outward to serve from the corporate discipline of expectant worship.

_____

_____

_____

Stewardship is the point of view that holds that all of creation is beholden to God the Creator. As human beings made in the image of God and given reason and other gifts, like imagination and the capacity for worship, we are given responsibility to stay mindfully aware of the origin of all things, and of our shared inheritance as created beings. If we hold a stewardship view of life, we believe that all that we have is from God, and therefore is or ought to be available to God's purposes.

_____

_____

_____

Gifts are individual characteristics, skills, and activities that are freely given. When speaking of spiritual gifts, we mean freely given gifts that are from God and presumably to be available to God's purposes. When considering one's own gifts, it may be helpful to consider not only things that seem "miraculous" and beyond one's own abilities, but also deeply rooted desires and concerns which may indicate an as-yet unknown calling. As Friends, we have inherited a rich tradition of universal ministry, which grew out of the Protestant reformation. It was the certainty of Christ's availability to all that gave George Fox and the others the courage and desire to worship in assemblies where it was acknowledged that God could use anyone at any time to carry forth God's purposes. Also of note, gifts may be given for a purpose or a time. It is never clear that a leading or gift is a lifetime commitment.

_____

_____

_____

Consulting Scripture

As you review these Bible verses, consider them in their larger context and notice any places where your understanding of obedience, discipleship, authority, worship, stewardship, and gifts/giftedness are expanded or challenged. Use the questions in the exercise that follows to focus your study. It may be helpful to read the passages before and after these excerpts to see them in their larger context.

Matthew 7:28-29

[28] Now when Jesus had finished saying these things, the crowds were astounded at his teaching, [29]for he taught them as one having authority, and not as their scribes.

Note: *These passages are from the New Revised Standard Version of the Bible, which is available in an easy-to-use, searchable format you can access at http://bible.oremus. org.*

Mark 6:7-11

[7]He called the twelve and began to send them out two by two, and gave them authority over the unclean spirits. [8]He ordered them to take nothing for their journey except a staff; no bread, no bag, no money in their belts; [9]but to wear sandals and not to put on two tunics. [10]He said to them, 'Wherever you enter a house, stay there until you leave the place. [11]If any place will not welcome you and they refuse to hear you, as you leave, shake off the dust that is on your feet as a testimony against them.'

Matthew 8:5-10

[5] When he entered Capernaum, a centurion came to him, appealing to him [6] and saying, 'Lord, my servant is lying at home paralyzed, in terrible distress.' [7] And he said to him, 'I will come and cure him.' [8] The centurion answered, 'Lord, I am not worthy to have you come under my roof; but only speak the word, and my servant will be healed. [9] For I also am a man under authority, with soldiers under me; and I say to one, "Go", and he goes, and to another, "Come", and he comes, and to my slave, "Do this", and the slave does it.' [10] When Jesus heard him, he was amazed and said to those who followed him, 'Truly I tell you, in no one in Israel have I found such faith.'

Luke 4:5-7

[5] Then the devil led him up and showed him in an instant all the kingdoms of the world. [6] And the devil said to him, 'To you I will give their glory and all this authority; for it has been given over to me, and I give it to anyone I please. [7] If you, then, will worship me, it will all be yours.'

Questions for reflecting on "authority" in Scripture:

1. What does the word "authority" convey in each of these passages?

2. In each example, who has authority and from what is it derived?

3. What connection do you see between authority and power, and authority and obedience?

4. What characteristics of discipleship are illustrated in any of these passages?

Insights from the Wider World of Friends, Past and Present

Read these thoughts from Friends and consider the questions that follow.

Early Friends refused to acknowledge the authority of kings and magistrates. They would quake only before God. They tried to recognize God's message in the speaking or actions of any spirit-centered person, regardless of his or her station in life. The gift of leadership was recognized in those who seemed best able to discern God's leadings for the group. Leadership was first and foremost a spiritual matter.[4]

---

[4] Bruce Birchard, "The Dilemmas of Organizational Leadership in the Religious Society of Friends," *Resources for Fostering Vital Friends Meetings*; available from

Friends have the practice of officially recognizing a gift in the ministry when a member has consistently spoken to the edification and spiritual help of the meeting…When a member gives evidence of such a gift, Ministry and Counsel may consider whether official recognition should be given. It should be borne in mind that such recognition in ministry not only is an expression of approval of one who is locally helpful but also is an affirmation of the Friend's ability to interpret the Society of Friends to the wider community.[5]

God, as understood in the Judeo-Christian tradition, works with and through his chosen people to carry out the divine plan for this part of creation on which we live. In a clearly subordinate way, we become co-workers with God to bring the world close to its intended condition. To accomplish this, God bestows on each faith community the spiritual gifts that community needs to do God's will. Not all gifts are given to all persons, nor are they given in the same measure to all those who receive them; but in total, the spiritual gifts that have been given are adequate to the share of the divine task that has been entrusted to each faith community.[6]

---

http://www.fgcquaker.org/library/fosteringmeetings/0402.html; Internet; accessed11 September 2007.

[5] New England Yearly Meeting, *Faith and Practice of New England Yearly Meeting of Friends* (Worcester, MA: New England Yearly Meeting of Friends,1985), 246.

[6] Lloyd Lee Wilson, *Essays on the Quaker Vision of Gospel Order* (Philadelphia: Quaker Press of Friends General Conference, 2002) 91.

After I had received that opening from the Lord, that to be bred at Oxford or Cambridge, was not sufficient to fit a man to be a minister of Christ, I regarded the priests less, and looked more after the dissenting people. Among them I saw there was some tenderness; and many of them came afterwards to be convinced, for they had some openings. But as I had forsaken the priests, so I left the separate preachers also, and those called the most experienced people; for I saw there was none among them all that could speak to my condition. And when all my hopes in them and in all men were gone, so that I had nothing outwardly to help me, nor could tell what to do; then, Oh! then I heard a voice which said, 'There is one, even Christ Jesus, that can speak to thy condition.' When I heard it, my heart did leap for joy. Then the Lord let me see why there was none upon the earth that could speak to my condition, namely, that I might give him all the glory. For all are concluded under sin, and shut up in unbelief, as I had been, that Jesus Christ might have pre-eminence, who enlightens, and gives grace, faith, and power. Thus when God doth work, who shall let it? This I knew experimentally.[7]

Reflecting with Friends

The complexity of Friends' experience is evident in the preceding passages, which all touch on some aspect of the vocabulary of faith and practice we have been exploring in these exercises. Consider the following

---

[7] George Fox, "A Journal Or Historical Account Of The Life, Travels, Sufferings, Of George Fox" in *The Works of George Fox*, vol. 2 (Philadelphia; New York: Marcus T.C. Gould, 1831), 74.

questions while reflecting on the passages above. Make note of any further questions you would like to explore on these topics.

1. What is the relationship between the "authority of kings and magistrates" and the authority Friends afford to individuals and organizations?

2. How does the recording process practiced in your yearly meeting relate to authority, consistency of giftedness, the ability of the recorded minister to represent and interpret the message of the Religious Society of Friends to the wider community?

3. How does your (or any) worshiping community identify its work in "the divine task" and how does identifying gifts tie in with identifying a community's mission?

4. In imagining a life of radical faithfulness, George Fox stood aside from recognizing formal education as a sufficient qualification to be a minister. In the oft-quoted passage from his journal cited above, how does the availability of Christ as teacher relate to formal education and experience? How do you imagine the world Fox worked in as similar to and dissimilar to the present day?

In Your Worship Community

Consider the following questions with other members of your community. Notice what use if any is made of the vocabulary that began this study: obedience, discipleship, authority, worship, stewardship, gifts/giftedness.

1. How is power or authority known in your meeting/church? What are the characteristics of those who are seen to speak with authority?

2. What role does obedience play in discipleship?

3. In what way is Jesus' authority similar to or related to the authority of leaders you have experienced?

4. Can you think of time when you were personally challenged to be obedient? Can you recall the sense of being called toward an obedient response? What was it like? How did you recognize it as a call to obedience?

CHAPTER TWO

The Biblical Tradition of Call

Called How and to What?

Living in relationship with God means that we seek parallels between our lives and the lives told in the Bible. We should remember, however, that the Bible not only provides wisdom and models for living, but it also lays the foundation for how we understand our relationship with God. There is a consistency between our lives and the lives detailed in Scripture, and the most sought-after consistency is that we might read Scripture in the company of the same Spirit that accompanied those who wrote it. Inspired reading unlocks the treasures of inspired writing, and emphasizes Friends' understanding of living with expectancy of the availability and loving Presence of Christ with us.

In common usage, Incarnation describes the understanding of the pre-existing Word of God we learn about in the Gospel of John manifesting in the human realm as the man Jesus. The purpose of this incarnation is understood differently among Christians, with ideas of its purpose ranging from the feudal notion of satisfaction for human offense against God to the exemplar notion of Jesus as role model for a human life lived in loving response to the divine. What is widely agreed upon among Christians is that the nature of God is revealed as never before in the life and teachings of Jesus of Nazareth. Jesus reveals the fullest truth ever made known about God, and he does so in a human life, lived in a human body with all bodily sensations and experiences available to it.

Another meaning of *incarnation* for Christians to consider is the incarnation of the mystical body of Christ, initiated by Jesus who gathered the first community of disciples to himself. The mystical body spans time and geography, is comprised of the faithful, and is under the leadership of Christ. The diverse yet faithful body of believers seeks to live in response to the teachings and guidance of Christ who is present. Among Friends, we tap into this presence, and reinforce our faith in this presence by the consistent practice of expectancy in worship. We sit in expectancy of the direction/message/word from Christ.

According to the Oxford English Dictionary, incarnation is the "act of being made flesh... the putting into or assumption of a concrete or definite form." If read in reference to the life of Jesus, this definition affirms the importance of his life and teachings. This definition may also be read in reference to what is expected of the faithful— that their faith should assume a concrete or definite form.

As a group, the faithful are often referred to as "the Body of Christ," which means that when many or all are incarnating their faith, the body of Christ is becoming incarnate. Friends' understanding of Christ's Presence as Teacher enlivens this understanding to include the present leadership of Christ to this body. Through expectancy in worship, and a pervasive attitude of worship that extends beyond times of formal church attendance, Friends seek to be taught by Christ how to further the incarnation of Christ and the kingdom of God about which Jesus taught.

When "incarnation" is extended to include the "incarnation" of the Body of Christ as the collection of followers who respond to Christ as head of the body to which they belong, the story of the incarnation extends even further into both the present and future. It might be compared to an inflatable object being taken from its storage container and growing to a stature and fullness that would not allow the object to return to its container of origin.

At times we may be called to action directly by God. Other times, we may be called to action by others in our community. And still other times, we may be called to action by our interests that grow up into concern accompanied by a sense of duty. In whatever way we are called to action, we may imagine that it is Christ with us who reveals the kingdom and its "Gospel Order" and Christ with us who invites us to "incarnate" our faith in action.

How Does God Interact in the World?

How does God interact in the world? It may seem like an easy, strange, or even silly question, but at root, one's answer will indicate a great deal about the sense of expectancy one has in life and also the sense of possibility. For one who understands God primarily as Creator, to whom all existence is beholden, a posture of gratitude and a sense of right order may be prominent. For one who understands God as Redeemer, a sense of hope and dependency may be prevalent. In looking at these two examples, we may note that the second understanding, that of God as Redeemer implies a level of activity and availability of God in the world that is greater than a long-ago Creator. These two examples are just two to consider. Scripture reveals other views and images of God. As well, the life we live in relationship with Christ provides new insights into the amazing story of God's on-going relationship with humanity.

As a way to begin unpacking our images of God, please respond to the following:

1. List some verbs for God. "God _____." For example, *created, loves, inspires,* etc.

2. Select three verbs from the above list and give one example from Scripture of God doing this action. In other words, express some Biblical "evidence" for how you know this about God.

3. Use the same three verbs, or three different ones, and give one example for each of God doing this action in the world. These examples may be from your life or from any event that has happened during your lifetime.

Call Stories of Our Spiritual Ancestors

Some good advice about reading Scripture comes from the Faith and Practice of North Carolina Yearly Meeting FUM.

The chief objective of the Bible student should be to grasp spiritual truths and teachings as vital and life–giving realities rather than to regard them as matters only for intellectual or doctrinal discussion. He should accept with appreciation all fresh light thrown upon the biblical records but should remain assured

that the spiritual strength which he receives from
such study comes from a living communion with
Him of whom the records tell. They are an
inexhaustible treasury of spiritual truth, fitted to the
needs and problems of each age as it reinterprets and
appropriates the message for its own time. Their
words are words of life because they testify of Him
who is Life. In keeping them there is great reward.[1]

With this in mind, and with your verbs for God in
mind, begin the following exercise in Scripture study.
For this exercise you will need a Bible. If your group is
large enough, break into groups of 2-3 with each group
taking one of the stories from Scripture listed below. In
your group, have one person read aloud the verses, and
then together consider the questions that follow.
(Alternately, Friends working on this study alone can
pick one or do all four sections of Scripture using the
same questions for reflection.)

- Matthew 9:9—The call of Matthew the tax
  collector
- Jeremiah 1:4-10—The call of the prophet
  Jeremiah
- 1 Samuel 3:1-21—The call of Samuel, servant of
  Eli
- Matthew 16:13-20—The renaming of Simon son
  of Jonah to Simon Peter

---

[1] North Carolina Yearly Meeting of Friends (Friends United Meeting),
Faith and Practice: Book of Discipline (2004). Available from
http://www.ncym-fum.org/Faith&Practice/F&P-index.htm; Internet;
accessed 14 December 2007.

Questions for Reflection:

1. What is the person being called to?

2. How does the call happen? What persons are involved and what discernment tools are used?

3. Imagine that you are the person receiving the call: what doubts, questions, and areas of resistance might you experience?

4. How is God present in the call narrative? Who else is present?

5. What is the role of community in each person's call and ministry?

Called by Community

While personal faith and involvement are essential to claiming a Christian identity, the idea that the faithful comprise and function as the Body of Christ means that community participation is vital to the life of faith. In practice, there may be bumps along the road to working together as one body, but we have encouragement to travel this road from stories about the earliest followers of Jesus.

After the resurrection and ascension, Peter addressed a crowd of 120 disciples. Citing that David had written prophetically about the betrayal committed by Judas, he concluded that, as in that writing by David, someone must take the job left behind by Judas.

Acts 1:21-26 describes the process of choosing between two disciples. The first criterion, met by both Barsabbas and Matthias, was that they were present at the baptism of Jesus by John and also witnessed the resurrection. Beyond that single requirement, the disciples were uncertain which of these two followers should take the place of Judas who had betrayed Jesus and was no longer among the disciples. They prayed to God, and relying on God's knowledge of every human heart, asked God to show them which to choose. They used the method of casting lots, which was an acceptable tool for discernment in that day and culture.

Although most nominating committees don't function this way today (drawing names!), there are important lessons to learn from this example in the early church:

- The needs of the community are taken into account.
- The process followed (casting lots after prayer) is a recognized tool of discernment in the community.
- There are basic requirements that candidates for the position must meet.

Sharing a Call Story

How do you recognize a calling and what are the earmarks of a divinely issued call? Before proceeding, read Matthew 5:14-16, which is the call of the church as a people to be light to the world. In some sense, all Christians are called to respond to the presence of Christ. Some have dramatic call experiences, as we often see exemplified in Scripture. Some have a subtler sense of divine guidance, as Rufus Jones reports:

> I had no ecstatic experiences, I was subject to no miraculous-seeming revelations, no sharp break occurred in the unfolding steps of a normal and ordinary life....I have few epoch-dates to record and no single Damascus vision. What I do feel sure of, however, is a frequent influx of divine life and power—the warm intimate touch of a guiding Hand. I somehow felt all through those college years that I was being prepared for something.[2]

Given that one may be called into action—into visibly manifesting their faith for the building up of the Body of Christ— by direct encounter with God, in response to community discernment, or in response to a deeply-seeded leading, most persons who are active in a faith community will be able to recollect some encounter that felt directive or encouraging. Take a few moments to consider your own experience, and in the space below, make a few notes.

A time when I felt led or called by God to a particular action was…

_____

_____

_____

---

[2] Rufus M. Jones, *The trail of life in college* (1929),135-136, cited in New England Yearly Meeting, *Faith and Practice*, 24.

A time when I felt led or called to a particular action
or activity and knew this call because of others in my
community expressing a need was....

_____

_____

_____

A time when I felt led or called by an urge or concern
welling up in me was...

_____

_____

_____

Insights from the Wider World of Friends, Past and Present

Read these thoughts from Friends, and consider the questions that follow.

From the early days of the Quaker movement Friends have insisted that a call to the ministry is of divine origin; that only the Holy Spirit ordains for service; that in no way is it transmitted by any human liturgical process, or human succession. The recording of ministers in the Society of Friends is simply the official recognition of that which has already occurred through the action of the Holy Spirit.[3]

From the glossary of the Book of Discipline of Iowa Yearly Meeting of Friends (Conservative):

To proceed as way opens—This means to wait for guidance, to avoid hasty judgment or action, to wait for future circumstances to help solve a problem. The spiritual guidance which may come is referred to as a "leading." Leadings may come in a time of seeking or entirely unexpectedly, bringing suggestions for previously unforeseen action.[4]

---

[3] Seth B. Hinshaw, *The Spoken Ministry Among Friends: Three Centuries of Progress and Development* (Davidson, North Carolina: North Carolina Yearly Meeting and North Carolina Friends Historical Society,1987), 56.
[4] Iowa Yearly Meeting of Friends (Conservative), *Book of Discipline*; available from http://www.quakernet.org/Discipline%201974/glossary__quaker.htm ; Internet; accessed 15 December 2007.

Reflecting with Friends

1. Can you recall an interaction with a Friend in meeting whom you recognize as one who ministers in such a way that the touch of the Holy Spirit on his or her life is evident? How have you known this person is a minister without knowing his or her "call story"? Consider asking this minister to tell you about his or her call to ministry.

2. Can you think of a story from Scripture of one whose call story we don't hear, but who is clearly being influenced in role or action by the Holy Spirit?

3. Looking over the notes made in answer to the first two questions in this section, can you imagine how the Holy Spirit is at work in your life?

In Your Worship Community

Consider the following question with other members of your community.

Do we have in place a way for those in ministry roles to share the story of their unfolding sense of calling to that service with the meeting? If not, can we initiate this kind of storytelling time?

CHAPTER THREE

Callings, Concerns, and Clearness Committees

Story is a powerful tool. One reason Christians respect and relate to Scripture as a source of authority is that the Bible tells the story of the relationship between God and humanity. Reading the history of our relationship with God offers an invitation and a reminder to be active in that relationship. Once the power of story is recognized, it is possible to move to the specific lessons revealed in the narrative.

Early Friends believed in the possibility of Christian perfection. Because Christ was the second Adam, all who were born into Christ—baptized by the Spirit—were born of Christ, and not of Adam. That the Son of God came to Earth is important, but how and when is less important. The experience of responding to this Presence is more important than doctrine about the details. Because the important elements in the life of Jesus (such as baptism, communion, healing, teaching) are part of an internal reality in individual disciples, it is the Seed of Christ, present in all humanity, that is able to respond to God. Christ in the believer brings the believer closer to God, as a tiny homing device or magnet would with the power not only to draw one closer to God but also to draw things out of alignment with God's will back toward God's will.

Friends have a long history of social activism and seeking to bring *Kingdom solutions* and ideals to the world. In a very real way, this is incarnation. The Kingdom of God manifests in the world whenever creation behaves in a way that is consistent with the loving intentions of God, which we are invited to know through the life and teachings of Jesus and the experience of the resurrected Christ. In fact, seeking Kingdom solutions may be the most natural unfolding of the work of *becoming* started by the life of Jesus, and continued in the resurrection and dispensing of the Holy Spirit. However, by disconnecting good works, Kingdom solutions, and Friends testimonies from the concept of incarnation, Friends disengage from the sturdy taproot of their spiritual heritage, and perhaps even from effectively internalizing the life of Jesus that was given as encouragement and instruction toward giving rise to the Kingdom within.

When early Friends stood in opposition to their Puritan colleagues, the Church of England, and the Roman Church, they were posing a re-reading of the second covenant. By insisting on the primacy of Christ's real presence in practices not controlled or authorized by a church body, they were insisting on the continuing revelation of God and the possibility of universal human responsiveness in spite of universal sinfulness.

The fact that Jesus, God's Word, is known to us through a life, which is known to us through narrative forms—words— indicates the power of story. Unlike memorized creeds, engaging a story invites the observer into relationship with the narrative and its contents. Time unfolds in stories, and between a reader/viewer and the narrative. Inviting the Holy Spirit to be with us in devotional reading and being able to reflect and be responsive to Scripture allows the effect of the gospel story to deepen and broaden over time as those who witness the story are changed by it. When we read Scripture as Friends, we have the lens of Friends tradition, and God willing, the assistance of the Holy Spirit, to open the gospel to us in ways that invite us to action on behalf of the Kingdom.

Coming into full awareness of the implications of Christian identity, one may realize that being a Christian is not confirmed by completing items on a checklist, but by living each moment with acknowledgement and striving toward the way of being taught by Jesus. Early Friend Robert Barclay describes his convincement this way:

> In part this is how I came to be a true witness. For it was not by the strength of arguments, or by the formal discussion of each doctrine in order to convince my understanding, that I came to receive and bear witness to my truth. Rather it was by being mysteriously reached by this life. For when I came into the silent assemblies of God's people, I felt a secret power among them, which touched my heart. And as I gave way to it, I found the evil in me weakening, and the good lifted up. Thus it was that I was knit into them and united with them. And I hungered more and more for the increase of this power and life until I could feel myself perfectly redeemed.[1]

For Barclay, convincement is definitely not an intellectual acceptance of wisdom or of persuasive

---

[1] Robert Barclay, *Barclay's Apology in Modern English*, ed. Dean Freiday (Philadelphia: Philadelphia and New York Yearly Meetings, 1967), 254.

arguments. He writes of the power of the silence and his reaction to it. On an internal level, perhaps unperceived by others, he felt his inner sinful nature receding under obedience to Christ. He then notes a hunger for more and a desire to be redeemed, to the state of pre-Fall perfection George Fox believed was possible. In his footnote to this section of Barclay's *Apology*, editor Dean Freiday expands the reader's historical understanding of Barclay's statement in its context.

> 'Convincement' preceded repentance (or 'self-conviction') in the early Friends consideration of the way in which one became a follower of Christ. ... 'Conversion,' which involved a conscious turning toward God, sometimes followed, but for others it did not.... Some modern Quaker usage [1967 edition] has oversimplified this, referring only to 'convincement' and disdaining the use of 'conversion,' which some other religious groups have abused into a sort of 'catching' of instant religion. The Friends refer instead to 'convincement' as the initial step on the long road to Christian perfection.[2]

If we pause to consider our own convincement as the moment or collection of moments in which we come to know that Christ is God in the world, and that we are continuously called to action, "conversion" becomes the opportunity available every moment of our lives as we try to live according to God's Truth. It is our unfolding conversion then that requires attention and discernment,

---

[2] Ibid., 254.

and given that this every-moment opportunity is the path to Christian living, seeking clearness through discernment is an essential Christian spiritual practice.

Questions for Reflection:

1. How do you experience Christ as Teacher or as the Word of God?

2. How do you recognize Christ and the Holy Spirit in your life?

3. How do you make the Teacher-disciple relationship manifest in the world and in your life (or the life of the meeting)?

4. What regular spiritual practices do you have as an individual or as part of your worship community that help you stay grounded for the work of living into your conversion on a daily basis?

5. When seeking to let your life speak, whose Word is being spoken? What is the evidence in your life of your reading of the Gospel?

Terms of Discernment

Calling	Leading	Clearness
Clearness Committee	Discernment	Concern

This chapter offers the chance to look at Friends understandings of discernment. As discussed in the previous chapter, the way one has experienced or come to know "evidence" of God's interaction in the world indicates how that person apprehends God's work in the world.

Edit and/or add to the definitions below to make them match your understanding.

Calling is a term to describe one's divinely-seeded invitation to formal ministry. Most often used as a noun, it is implied that God calls, and the faithful respond.

_____

_____

_____

Leading, like calling, describes a divinely seeded invitation to ministry. Often used for less formal ministry roles, it is often used as a verb, as in "I feel led to do X." There are several tests for confirming that a leading is from God and not from one's ego. Among these is the requirement that it be tested against Scripture and not found in conflict, and also that one's community prayerfully consider and affirm the leading.

_____

_____

_____

Concern as a noun indicates an area of need in the world, for which a deep passion and worry is planted in a person's heart. It is often accompanied by or comes into being accompanied by a sense of obligation to act to address the area of need. Often meeting and church corporate outreach ministries grow out of shared concern.

_____

_____

_____

Discernment is a process of consideration that begins with an idea or urge that is refined by prayer and community reflection. It is an intentional decision-making process that unfolds on "God time" and may resemble a kind of "excavation" of the movement of Christ in one's life or in the life of the meeting.

_____

_____

_____

The clearness committee is a Friends practice, originally used for consideration of marriage and meeting membership, but now also used for other decisions. Clearness is the sought-after state which is known by a deep peace and dissolution of worry about the path to be taken. Clearness committees are sometimes appointed by a meeting or convened by the person in the process of discernment. Usually 3-5 spiritually wise Friends coming from diverse life experiences meet once or twice to prayerfully reflect with the focus person by posing deepening questions.

_____

_____

_____

Consulting Scripture

Consider Acts 15. In this chapter, the disciples must address the question of what the Jewish followers of Jesus are to require of Gentile believers. After community deliberation, it is decided that three areas of observance must be kept by Gentile believers.

Acts 15:1-35

Then certain individuals came down from Judea and were teaching the brothers, 'Unless you are circumcised according to the custom of Moses, you cannot be saved.' [2]And after Paul and Barnabas had no small dissension and debate with them, Paul and Barnabas and some of the others were appointed to go up to Jerusalem to discuss this question with the apostles and the elders. [3]So they were sent on their way by the church, and as they passed through both Phoenicia and Samaria, they reported the conversion of the Gentiles, and brought great joy to all the believers. [4]When they came to Jerusalem, they were welcomed by the church and the apostles and the elders, and they reported all that God had done with them. [5]But some believers who belonged to the sect of the Pharisees stood up and said, 'It is necessary for them to be circumcised and ordered to keep the law of Moses.'
[6] The apostles and the elders met together to consider this matter. [7]After there had been much debate, Peter stood up and said to them, 'My brothers, you know that in the early days God made a choice among you, that I should be the one through whom the Gentiles would hear the message of the good news and become believers. [8]And God, who knows the human heart, testified to them by giving them the Holy Spirit, just as he did to us; [9]and in cleansing their hearts by faith he has made no distinction between them and us. [10]Now therefore why are you putting God to the test by placing on the neck of the disciples a yoke that neither our ancestors nor we have been able to bear? [11]On the contrary, we believe that we will be saved through the grace of the Lord Jesus, just as they will.'

[12] The whole assembly kept silence, and listened to Barnabas and Paul as they told of all the signs and wonders that God had done through them among the Gentiles. [13]After they finished speaking, James replied, 'My brothers, listen to me. [14]Simeon has related how God first looked favourably on the Gentiles, to take from among them a people for his name. [15]This agrees with the words of the prophets, as it is written,
[16]"After this I will return,
and I will rebuild the dwelling of David, which has fallen;
   from its ruins I will rebuild it,
      and I will set it up,
[17]so that all other peoples may seek the Lord—
   even all the Gentiles over whom my name has been called.

   Thus says the Lord, who has been making these things [18]known from long ago."
[19]Therefore I have reached the decision that we should not trouble those Gentiles who are turning to God, [20]but we should write to them to abstain only from things polluted by idols and from fornication and from whatever has been strangled and from blood. [21]For in every city, for generations past, Moses has had those who proclaim him, for he has been read aloud every sabbath in the synagogues.'
[22] Then the apostles and the elders, with the consent of the whole church, decided to choose men from among their members and to send them to Antioch with Paul and Barnabas. They sent Judas called Barsabbas, and Silas, leaders among the brothers, [23]with the following letter: 'The brothers, both the apostles and the elders, to the believers of Gentile origin in Antioch and Syria and Cilicia, greetings. [24]Since we have heard that certain persons who have gone out from us, though with no instructions from us, have said things to disturb you and have unsettled your minds, [25]we have decided unanimously

[27]We have therefore sent Judas and Silas, who themselves will tell you the same things by word of mouth. [28]For it has seemed good to the Holy Spirit and to us to impose on you no further burden than these essentials: [29]that you abstain from what has been sacrificed to idols and from blood and from what is strangled and from fornication. If you keep yourselves from these, you will do well. Farewell.'

[30] So they were sent off and went down to Antioch. When they gathered the congregation together, they delivered the letter. [31]When its members read it, they rejoiced at the exhortation. [32]Judas and Silas, who were themselves prophets, said much to encourage and strengthen the believers. [33]After they had been there for some time, they were sent off in peace by the believers to those who had sent them. [35]But Paul and Barnabas remained in Antioch, and there, with many others, they taught and proclaimed the word of the Lord.

Note: *These passages are from the New Revised Standard Version of the Bible, which is available in an easy-to-use, searchable format you can access at http://bible.oremus.org.*

Questions for reflecting on community discernment in Scripture:

1. What is the issue and how has it come to light?

2. Who is involved in the discernment process?

3. What method is used to settle the issue?

Insights from the Wider World of Friends, Past and Present

Read these thoughts from Friends, and consider the questions that follow.

The concept of holy obedience is predicated on the faith that the divine will may be ascertained when the human heart is sufficiently attuned and receptive. This concept is fundamental to the Quaker way of life and worship. Holy obedience would be a meaningless term apart from the faith that God is in fact seeking those who will worship him in spirit and in truth, and that he does reveal his holy will to those who will seek diligently for it. On the basis of experience, Quakers declare that man does have a capacity to comprehend divine revelation, and thus to enter into communion with his Creator and Redeemer.[3]

The relationship between individuals and community has always been complex in Quakerism. The pendulum has swung back and forth in each chapter of Quaker history in an effort to avoid the extremes of anarchy and rigidity. There must be enough freedom so that the individual can be truly open to divine leadings because Friends hold that revelation is a continuing process, that God can lead people into

---

[3]Hinshaw, *The Spoken Ministry Among Friends*, 8.

new truths, especially in matters of ethics or morality. At the same time, there is a need for sufficient structure to preserve the tradition that has valued that freedom. Leadings come to individuals, but the group discerns whether they are genuine. [4]

The Quaker use of the word 'concern' reflects our understanding about how God works through humans: it is a key element of Quaker spirituality, by which the Spirit engages with the world in creation, mercy, testimony, action. In the matrix of prayer, or in some other way, a matter comes before your mind which feels important, urgent or pre-possessing. ... A concern is more than subject matter, however, more than an area of interest or passion, because it is accompanied (sooner or later) by a sense of duty: something is required, and at the Lord's hand.[5]

'Concern' is a word which has tended to become debased by excessively common usage among Friends, so that too often it is used to cover merely a strong desire. The true 'concern' [emerges as] a gift from God, a leading of his spirit which may not be denied. Its sanction is not that on investigation it proves to be the intelligent thing to do – though it usually is; it is that the individual ... knows, as a matter of inward experience, that there is something that the Lord would have done, however obscure the way,

---

[4] Michael Birkel, *Silence and Witness: The Quaker Tradition*, (Maryknoll, New York: Orbis Books, 2004), 55.
[5] Drayton, *On Living With A Concern For Gospel Ministry*, 24.

however uncertain the means to human observation. Often proposals for action are made which have every appearance of good sense, but as the meeting waits before God it becomes clear that the proposition falls short of 'concern'.[6]

A kindred voice outside the Society:

A note on the activity of the Spirit in the self is important. The Holy Spirit joins our human spirit; it does not replace it. We humans enjoy three modes of activity flowing from the three dimensions of our being—body, mind, spirit. It is helpful to imagine three concentric circles: the center is the spirit, the middle is the mind, the outer is the body. Every human activity engages all three levels. Our physical and psychological activities are obvious to all. But what are our spiritual activities? The spiritual level is the level of our freedom, our freedom to respond to the Spirit or not to respond. The Holy Spirit joins our human spirit, initiating within us the desire for goodness—without the Spirit's presence we would not even have the desire. Responding to the Spirit then transforms the other levels of our being, the physical and the psychological. The Spirit is the principle for all Christian life. Traditionally this indwelling of the Spirit has been called 'sanctifying

---

[6] Roger Wilson (1949), cited in Yearly Meeting of the Religious Society of Friends (Quakers) in Britain, *Quaker Faith and Practice*, Third ed.(London: Quaker Books, 2005), 13.07. Available from http://quakersfp.live.poptech.coop/qfp/chap13/13.02.html#13.05; Internet; accessed 15 December 2007.

grace.' Christian discernment seeks to recognize this Spirit and respond to it.[7]

Reflecting with Friends

1. In considering "holy obedience" and the ability to know divine will, what are the best ways you have known to ascertain that God's will is being pursued in your life or your meeting?

2. Regarding community discernment, in your experience, does it seem that community is more often involved in positive encouragement or in monitoring against ego-driven or misled leadings?

3. Can you recall your involvement in a concern being brought for consideration before the larger community? It may be an issue in business meeting or an individual concern brought for confirmation by the meeting. What process brought the concern to the larger body?

---

[7] Richard J. Hauser, S.J., "Each Mortal Thing Does One Thing and the Same—Selves: An Approach to Christian Discernment" in vol. 3 of *Handbook of Spirituality for Ministers*, ed. Robert J. Wicks (New York: Paulist Press, 1995), 211.

In Your Worship Community

Consider the following questions with other members of your community.

1. How does the yearly meeting book of discipline describe the work of the nominating committee? Do words or concepts like *holy obligation, gospel, kingdom, clearness,* and *discernment* figure into the process, in writing or in practice?

2. In your meeting or church, what does the typical request for one to be in service sound like? Write out or "perform" a role play of this process with others watching. Consider ways the conversation could be re-framed to grow from the encouragement of testing leadings or from the invitation to respond to the Gospel in one's life.

3. Have Friends in your meeting share an experience of determining to accept a request for service or to decline one. Suggest that the details of prayer, mentoring and community reflection be highlighted where they exist.

CHAPTER FOUR

Identifying Gifts and Needs in/for the Body

Earlier in our study we touched on the topic of ministry. When we talk about gifts, or even about skills, we, as a Religious Society, are talking about ministry. In this context, another word for ministry is witness. One way of understanding "witness" is as our response to our experience of God as it is observable to others in our life on earth. In some basic sense, Christian identity is not a check-list of accomplishments or beliefs, rather it is an orientation to a way of being that is in response to the truth one comes to know through experiencing the living Christ.

Body of Christ is a term with a wide variety of understandings among persons of faith. Paul, at the end of 1 Corinthians 12, describes the body of Christ as a countercultural entity in which assumptions may cloud understanding. This passage immediately precedes the oft quoted passage about love in 1 Corinthians 13, which is the "better way" Paul refers to in the final verse cited. He recommends striving for the greater gifts among those he lists, then he declares that love is a better way even beyond those.

[27]Now you are the body of Christ and individually members of it. [28]And God has appointed in the church first apostles, second prophets, third teachers; then deeds of power, then gifts of healing, forms of assistance, forms of

leadership, various kinds of tongues. [29]Are all apostles? Are all prophets? Are all teachers? Do all work miracles? [30]Do all possess gifts of healing? Do all speak in tongues? Do all interpret? [31]But strive for the greater gifts. And I will show you a still more excellent way. [1]

Pause from reading and read the end of 1 Corinthians 12 and Chapter 13.

Consider this advice from Paul alongside the idea that your meeting is part of the larger Body of Christ, and that in some ways, the witness of your meeting to the community is the witness of a free-standing incarnation of the Body. So, while work must be done, committees named and held accountable, the evangelist echoes the greatest commandment when he says that love is greater still.

This study is about the nuts and bolts of gifts and meeting needs, but the consideration of these applications may be best grounded in our understandings of what it means to witness in the world.

---

[1] 1 Corinthians 12:27-31. This passage is from the New Revised Standard Version of the Bible, which is available in an easy-to-use, searchable format you can access at *http://bible.oremus.org*.

Terms of Ministry

Witness	Ministry	Body of Christ	Membership

Read the explanations of terms offered below and add to them as needed. In the space that follows, make note of any new questions rising in you that you would like to explore with others in your meeting.

Witness is the response of a person of faith to her/his experience of God; usually this response is evident to others who encounter this person. Among some Friends, the phrase "Let your life speak" captures the essence of applied Christian ethics. Witness further describes the striving of a person to live with integrity and to participate in God's work in the world as a way of responding to one's encounter with God.

_____

_____

_____

Ministry is a term that refers to actions taken in the world to bring the world into alignment with God's intention for the world. This may be seen as a formal and intentional "witness" (see above) that is offered with consistency and/or as a named activity (e.g., chaplaincy, pastoral ministry, spiritual direction, teaching, healing, etc.). Much ministry is modeled after Scripture, the early church, and Christians in history. Among Friends, *vocal ministry* is a term for spoken messages delivered during expectant worship. Sometimes one is called to a life ministry and other times to a ministry for a particular occasion. An issue currently facing the church, and the Religious Society of Friends, is defining the needs and vision for ministry in the 21st century. "Where does God call us to be, and how will we get there from here?"

_____

_____

_____

Membership is the condition of being formally joined to a group or meeting. Various books of discipline recommend that members be active volunteers and/or support the work of the meeting financially. Joining a particular monthly and yearly meeting means that one finds oneself to be in unity with that meeting's interpretation of Friends faith and practice.

_____

_____

_____

Membership in the Body of Christ acknowledges one to be in relationship to the living Christ, and recognizes that one is in this relationship with others who are also in relationship to Christ.

_____

_____

_____

List any questions you would like to consider further with members of your meeting:

_____

_____

_____

How the Work Gets Done

A boy told his friend a joke like this: There was a frog sitting beside a pond catching and eating flies. He would snap his tongue out to catch a fly, and with each success, he would pause to laugh. Another frog came by and asked the first frog what he was doing. "Catching flies. Want to join me?" So, the two of them started catching flies, and pausing between successful attempts, laughed heartily. A third frog came down the path and asked the first two what they were doing. "Catching flies. Want to join us?" While they waited for his reply, the two resumed their catch-and-giggle rhythm. The third frog said, "What's so funny about catching flies? The first frog said, "Time's fun when you're catching flies."

This play on words offers two lessons. Vocabulary matters, because it is the common ground of understanding that is both the content and form of communication. And, changing one's perspective on a task or role can open new possibilities to that person and to others who witness the changed perspective.

In some meetings, the work of nominating committee takes on the look of recruiting to fill vacancies. In jest, it may be called, "the arm-twisting committee." Let us examine the difference between a recruiting model and a leadership development model.

Add additional characteristics that come to mind in the space provided.

Leadership development focused meeting:

- o Vocabulary of encouragement
- o "Recruiting" is personal and personalized
- o A dialogue approach in which gifts and needs are considered
- o Volunteers are spiritually fed by their work/ministry

_____

_____

_____

Recruiting focused meeting:

- o Vocabulary of obligation, need and lack
- o Public pleas to fill vacancies
- o Harried/guilty feeling nominating committee
- o Volunteers may be tired or overdone on specific tasks

_____

_____

_____

Take a few minutes to answer the following questions about your meeting.

1. Has your personal experience of volunteering in your meeting felt more often like you were recruited, or more often like your leadership gifts were being encouraged? What are some characteristics of each from your point of view as a recruitee/leader-in-formation?

_____

_____

_____

2. If you have served on a nominating committee or its equivalent, describe some of your best experiences and some of your challenges.

_____

_____

_____

Consulting Scripture

Consider the following passages from Scripture and in the space provided below, summarize the point of what is being taught by the author.

[3]For by the grace given to me I say to everyone among you not to think of yourself more highly than you ought to think, but to think with sober judgment, each according to the measure of faith that God has assigned. [4]For as in one body we have many members, and not all the members have the same function, [5]so we, who are many, are one body in Christ, and individually we are

members one of another. [6]We have gifts that differ according to the grace given to us: prophecy, in proportion to faith; [7]ministry, in ministering; the teacher, in teaching; [8]the exhorter, in exhortation; the giver, in generosity; the leader, in diligence; the compassionate, in cheerfulness. [2]

What advice would Paul be offering to a modern-day nominating committee or worship community?

[7]But each of us was given grace according to the measure of Christ's gift. ... [11]The gifts he gave were that some would be apostles, some prophets, some evangelists, some pastors and teachers, [12]to equip the saints for the work of ministry, for building up the body of Christ, [13]until all of us come to the unity of the faith and of the knowledge of the Son of God, to maturity, to the measure of the full stature of Christ. [14]We must no longer be children, tossed to and fro and blown about by every wind of doctrine, by people's trickery, by their craftiness in deceitful scheming. [15]But speaking the truth in love, we must grow up in every way into him who is the head, into Christ, [16]from whom the whole body, joined and knitted together by every ligament with which it is equipped, as each part is working properly, promotes the body's growth in building itself up in love. [3]

---

[2] Romans 12:3-8.
[3] Ephesians 4:7, 11-16.

What advice would Paul be offering to a modern-day nominating committee or worship community?

> [7]The end of all things is near; therefore be serious and discipline yourselves for the sake of your prayers. [8]Above all, maintain constant love for one another, for love covers a multitude of sins. [9]Be hospitable to one another without complaining. [10]Like good stewards of the manifold grace of God, serve one another with whatever gift each of you has received. [11]Whoever speaks must do so as one speaking the very words of God; whoever serves must do so with the strength that God supplies, so that God may be glorified in all things through Jesus Christ. To him belong the glory and the power for ever and ever. Amen.[4]

What advice would Peter be offering to a modern-day nominating committee or worship community?

---

[4] 1 Peter 4:7-11.

Insights from the Wider World of Friends, Past and Present

Read these thoughts from Friends and consider the questions that follow.

> Friends hold in special esteem the gift qualifying
> for the ministry. They do not ordain ministers,
> but as the gift develops and obedience to the
> Holy Spirit is manifest, they recognize the gift
> and encourage its training and exercise. There is a
> variety of ministries: evangelism; exposition and
> teaching of the gospel truths; engaging in prayer
> and in praise; exhortation and encouragement;
> speaking to states and conditions; and pastoral
> care. No sharp line of distinction can be drawn
> between the different types of ministry; all may be
> cultivated and developed by prayerful study and
> close observation of human need.[5]

> When a member has frequently spoken to the
> spiritual needs of himself and fellow worshipers,
> Friends should encourage him/her in this service. If
> this person continues to grow in the ministry, the
> Meeting should recognize this gift by recording him
> or her as a minister.[6]

---

[5] North Carolina Yearly Meeting of Friends (Friends United Meeting), *Faith and Practice*, "Gift of the Ministry," 33.
[6] Iowa Yearly Meeting of Friends (Conservative), *Faith and Practice*, "Recording of Ministers."

Reflecting with Friends

1. What in the passages above resonates or echoes what you believe about Friends and ministry?

2. Does your meeting (yearly or monthly) have a statement on ministry, universal ministry, recording ministers, etc.? Take a moment to review your meeting's book of discipline to see what is written there on these things.

3. How does the practical demonstration of ministry and leadership development in your meeting reflect what is written in the book of discipline? What changes would you make to this section of the book of discipline if given the task?

Universal Ministry: Differentiation of Function while Maintaining Unity

Friends have a long history of the sense of universal ministry. It began with George Fox's assertion that the Church of England with all its hierarchy did not have a special connection to God that was inaccessible except through the church. Because anyone at any time may have an experience of the Inward Teacher's influence, anyone at anytime may be called to live and act in response to that encounter. This is universal ministry at its root. Universal ministry does not mean that anyone is suited for any task at anytime. The deep but subtle difference between these two understandings is that God calls persons to action, and these actions are part of a person's witness to his or her faith. Elements of a person's witness may take the form of ministry, and be directed within the meeting or outward toward the wider community. When a purpose-driven recruitment model is followed, it is possible that the call and response song with God is inaudible or shouted down by arm-twisting.

This chapter addresses questions about gifts and needs within the context of the local congregation. In some ways, this may require an "owner occupied renovation" in which things that have always been or been seen a certain way, will have to be re-examined and confirmed. We will approach an assessment of meeting needs first, and then move to personal assessment of gifts. (Note that "gifts" may be naturally held inclinations or talents or skills that have been built over a lifetime. In the case of "skills," we may believe that the inclination and the aptitude are from God, and the skill-building we have done is our way of participating with and responding to God as we work toward manifesting the Body of Christ.) In both assessments, participants are encouraged to live close to the Voice that issues the Call. "Calling," like conversion, is a daily, lifelong pursuit that comes about in response to experiencing God's Presence.

Complete the inventory of meeting needs and individual gifts in Chapter Five.

In Your Worship Community

Queries for reflection:

- How do I/we imagine the Kingdom of God? Where do my/our gifts fit in and for the Kingdom?

- On the deepest level, do I/we regard my time and talents as gifts from God now in my care?

- How am I/are we demonstrating my/our faith with my/our use of time and gifts? How do others witness my/our faith by observing my/our life?

CHAPTER FIVE

Surveying the Body, Reflecting on the Call and the Tools Given for the Work

The following pages contain questions designed to help members of Friends meetings and churches look faithfully at the work they are called to and at the gifts and skills they have been given individually and collectively to make this work possible.

As Friends we believe in Christ's continuing presence with us, and our worship takes on the posture of expectancy. In worship and in life, we anticipate and become willing to be changed by those encounters with Christ. This willingness is the basis for discipleship— a life lived in response to the persistent presence of Christ the Teacher. As members of Friends meetings, we live collectively in worshipping communities, and we function as bodies of Christ, called to witness to our encounters with God by letting our corporate and individual lives speak of the amazing news of God's love as revealed in the life of Jesus.

Corporate Inventory

As you begin to consider the needs of your meeting community, pause for a moment to think about the long-held Friends' belief in universal ministry. This stems from the belief that God may make use of any person at any time for God's purposes. This puts the responsibility on the faithful to seek God's presence in any place at any time. It also requires that we understand the relationship between universal ministry and differentiation of gifts and tasks within a body. God may call anyone at anytime, but we must listen faithfully to insure that the call is authentic, to understand the structure of the body and to know our role in it.

A "becoming" is in process when Friends see themselves as a "body." We rely upon the personal encounter with Christ as the beginning of our convincement. This same personal encounter provides inspiration for our conversion process as we work to live in response to the truth learned through divine encounter. We believe we can be a new creation. This is a truth held individually and corporately. As you consider the following questions, be attentive to your thought process. What do your answers say or imply about the nature of the world, and about your meeting's relationship to the world? These underlying truths about the world and your meeting's place in it may be useful to share with others in your meeting.

This exercise is also a practical needs assessment for the meeting. There are some standard areas of ministry and administration that most churches and meetings need. Generally, they can be grouped into categories: pastoral care of the meeting, support of the pastoral minister, buildings and grounds, community outreach and service, peace and justice concerns, worship planning and support, financial stewardship and fundraising, teaching, and mentoring. *How can your meeting be a new creation and be an instrument for new creation in the wider world?*

Section 1

Consider this first set of questions by yourself. Make some notes and if time allows, share your answers with others in meeting. Otherwise, let the process of answering these questions prepare you for the group questions in Section 2.

1. Consider and rate the following aspects of your meeting community. Respond with your first thoughts on each, and give a numerical rating using the scale below. (An honest assessment of present conditions will be most useful in determining needs.)

Pastoral care of the meeting
(needs work)   1   2   3   4   5   (best)

Support of the pastoral minister
(needs work)   1   2   3   4   5   (best)

Buildings and grounds
(needs work)   1   2   3   4   5   (best)

Community outreach/invitation
(needs work)   1   2   3   4   5   (best)

Community service
(needs work)   1   2   3   4   5   (best)

Peace and justice concerns
(needs work)   1   2   3   4   5   (best)

Worship planning and support
(needs work)   1   2   3   4   5   (best)

Financial stewardship
(needs work)   1   2   3   4   5   (best)

Fundraising
(needs work)   1   2   3   4   5   (best)

Religious education
(needs work)   1   2   3   4   5   (best)

Spiritual mentoring/eldering
(needs work)   1   2   3   4   5   (best)

Encouragement of spiritual gifts
(needs work)   1   2   3   4   5   (best)

2. What do you enjoy most about your meeting?

3. What do you enjoy most about your First Day experience with your meeting?

4. What does your meeting do particularly well?

5. What does your meeting do poorly or not at all?

6. If you were inviting a non-Quaker friend to visit your meeting, what three things could you name as things this person might expect and enjoy?

    a.

    b.

    c.

Section 2

Consider the following questions, in order, with members of your meeting, allowing time for members to write down their answers. As Friends are willing, invite the group to share as a whole. It might be helpful to have a note-taker or recording clerk to collect the sense of this discussion.

1. If a genie appeared offering three wishes for the improvement of my meeting, I would ask for:

    a.

    b.

    c.

2. If the same genie came to meeting for worship for business with the same offer, the gathered group might ask for:

    a.

    b.

    c.

3. Where do your personal desires for the meeting match what you imagine the gathered membership at business meeting would ask for? Where do your desires differ?

Individual Inventory

As we become more at ease with the idea that we are part of a functioning body, we may be able to live more on faith—relinquishing certainty and strong will, and taking up a commitment to improve the spiritual life and practices of the community (the body) that we belong to. Expand your consideration from simply "What must be done?" to "What would I most love to do?" It may be helpful to consider your passions. Where do you find delight and joy? What activities seem to facilitate your increased awareness of God's presence? As you consider the following questions, pause to listen for the places where the answer is a clear "yes!"

What are you good at? What do other people tell you you're good at? Now that you have been thinking of your meeting as the Body of Christ, "incarnating" for a particular purpose, discernible by knowing the gifts, skills, joys and desires of the group, you are ready to explore where you fit in this body and with its purpose.

Where in the Body am I? And what am I for?

Check all that apply to you:

_____   I enjoy visiting with people in their homes.

_____   I am able to be cheerful and encouraging when others are plainly suffering.

_____   Friends tell me I am a "people person."

_____   I enjoy the time before and after worship because I like to mingle with f/Friends.

_____   I like making phone calls to check-in with others.

_____   Being hospitable is something that is very important to me, and/or I do it well.

_____   Given the choice of working with information or working with people, I would chose people without a second thought.

If you see many checks in this short list, you may be suited for "people care" and related ministries. These might include serving as a greeter, making visits to home-bound and hospitalized friends, or managing a congregational prayer list. What are some other ministries that fall under the category of "people care"?

_____

_____

_____

Check all that apply to you:

____   I don't have much time to help on a consistent basis.
____   I like to get really involved in a single project and then take a rest.
____   I am a natural entertainer.
____   I like to have people over for dinner parties.
____   Friends often look to me for help with weddings, showers, birthday parties, etc.
____   I am organized and enjoy being accurate with detail-oriented work.
____   I look forward to annual events and recurring traditions.

If you see many checks in this list, you may be suited to work on events and related ministries. These might be annual fundraising events, fellowship events, holiday parties, etc. Such commitments are short-term but intense, and may benefit from a continuity from year-to-year. What other needs are there in your worship community that fall under the broad category of events?

_____

_____

_____

Check all that apply to you:

_____   I enjoy working with my hands on practical tasks.
_____   The appearance of a building tells me a lot about
        what goes on inside it.
_____   I enjoy working with plants and landscaping.
_____   I enjoy home maintenance and home
        improvement projects.
_____   Others often ask for my advice or assistance with
        building and maintenance projects.
_____   I have a knack for fixing things.
_____   I like painting, inside or out.

If you see many checks in this list, you may be suited to work on care of buildings and grounds. Depending on the situation of your meeting, this could include inside and outside tasks, and could provide year-round opportunities. In addition to mowing grass, tending gardens, carpentry, and painting, what other skills, gifts and interests might suit a person for work related to buildings and grounds care?

_____

_____

_____

Check all that apply to you:

_____   The structure and flow of worship is important to
        me.
_____   I have a strong familiarity with Scripture and
        hymns and easily see where they match.

_____ I have gifts for preaching, but I wouldn't want to do it all the time.

_____ I tend to see the pastor as a person as well as a spiritual leader. I pray for him/her regularly.

_____ I enjoy singing.

_____ I have musical interests and talents that could be of use in worship.

_____ I am aesthetically inclined and can "set a space" that is inviting to the purpose.

If you see many checks in this list, you may be suited to work in the area of worship and worship planning. Depending on the organization of your meeting, this may include providing pulpit supply, serving on a pastoral support committee, arranging the worship space, participating in the choir or providing other music. What other ministries would be in the category of supporting the corporate worship experience of your meeting?

_____

_____

_____

Check all that apply to you:

_____ I am business minded and have experience in other organizations with financial concerns.

_____ I enjoy working with my home budget and accounts.

_____ I am willing to talk plainly with people about money and financial contributions.

_____ I am a good record-keeper.

_____ I enjoy the process of determining costs and timelines of projects.

_____ I have served on the board of a non-profit organization.

_____ Others come to me for advice on investments and major purchases.

If you see many checks in this list, you may be suited for ministry in the area of financial stewardship. This may include serving as treasurer or on an investments committee. It may include representing your meeting on the board of an organization supported by it. What other ministries would be in the category of supporting the financial stability of your worship community?

_____

_____

_____

Check all that apply to you:

_____ I have a natural inclination toward and enjoyment of prayer.

_____ I enjoy being with people one-on-one.

_____ Others tell me I am a good listener.

_____ I routinely have a sense of the general spiritual state of the meeting.

_____ I am particularly drawn to be a prayerful presence for the pastoral minister and other leaders.

_____ I would enjoy being on a committee whose purpose is spiritual care of the meeting.

_____ I am able to see and enjoy naming and nurturing spiritual gifts in others.

If you see many checks in this list, you may be suited for work that falls under the umbrella of pastoral care. Like the more general "people work" listed above, there are many possible outlets for these gifts. However, serving on a pastoral care committee may involve lots of prayer for members in need, and working with the larger committee to monitor and nurture the corporate spiritual life of the meeting and certain groups within (like youth, singles, elders, etc.) What other tasks and gifts might be in the category of pastoral care?

_____

_____

_____

Check all that apply to you:

____   I sense that I have been called to spiritual leadership of a group.
____   I enjoy preaching and can imagine doing so on a regular basis.
____   People seek my advice and counsel.
____   I am not threatened to stand alongside others in times of crisis and need.
____   I pray regularly for the meeting and for others.
____   I am energized by study and discipleship.
____   I can lead without needing to dominate decision-making.

If you see many checks in this list, it may be time to consider that you are called to pastoral ministry. While the lived job descriptions of Friends pastors vary from church to church, the gifts, skills and inclinations covered in this list are characteristics of successful pastors. What other gifts, skills, and interests make a good pastor?

_____

_____

_____

Check all that apply to you:

_____ Others tell me I have a gift for teaching.
_____ Others come to me with questions about religious topics.
_____ I have studied Scripture, history, spiritual disciplines, and/or other religious topics.
_____ I enjoy relaying complicated information in easily digestible form.
_____ Others tell me I am good at formulating questions.
_____ I enjoy ideas and talking with people about ideas.
_____ I am good at perceiving a person's learning style and needs.

If you see many checks in this list, it may be that you are called to teaching, either for adults or children. The work of religious education, theological reflection, and developing sustaining spiritual practices can be directed toward persons of any age. In addition to these areas, what others might fit into the category of education?

_____

_____

_____

Check all that apply to you:

_____   I have studied Quaker faith and practice and am very familiar with our yearly meeting's book of discipline.

_____   I enjoy talking to non-Quakers about what goes on in worship and about how my faith intersects with my life.

_____   I enjoy being with others who are not like me, and find these to be opportunities for mutually beneficial learning.

_____   I am a visible representative in my community for my meeting/church.

_____   People who know me at all know I am a member of my meeting/church. My involvement is fundamental to my identity.

_____   I am involved with the yearly meeting and quarterly meeting.

_____   People tell me I am good at explaining things to others outside of a group.

If you see many checks in this list, you may be suited to work that falls under the category of interpreting/outreach. Depending on your meeting's culture and sense of mission, this may include creating opportunities to speak with non-Friends about our faith and practice, or simply being deemed a fluent speaker of the language of faith and practice. In addition to having a sense of Quaker practice, history, relationship to Scripture, and vocabulary, what other tasks, gifts or skills might one called to interpreting the faith or to doing "outreach" need?

_____

_____

_____

Check all that apply to you:

____ People seek me out for private conversations about their spiritual journeys.

____ When I offer vocal ministry, people often approach me after worship to talk more about the message offered.

____ I am easily able to name and nurture gifts in others.

____ Sometimes I am led to approach others and start conversations in which my primary role is to offer reflective listening.

____ I sometimes feel a sense of inner prompting when people ask me a question.

____ People tell me that I am easy to trust and/or that they feel comfortable sharing with me.

____ Usually hearing about others' suffering is an invitation to prayerful consideration and does not drain me.

If you see many checks in this list, you may be called to be a mentor in a spiritual context. While many are accustomed to having a professional mentor to help them in their career journey, not many are accustomed to the presence of spiritual mentors. It may be that a mentor is a person a little further along on their journey with God, or a little more practiced at the discipline of seeking God. What other characteristics might make one

a spiritual mentor? What particular roles might such a
mentor fill in a monthly meeting?

_____

_____

_____

CHAPTER SIX

Styles and Models of Leadership

Earlier in our study we touched on the topic of ministry. When we talk about gifts, or even about skills, we, as a Religious Society, are talking about ministry. In this context, another word for ministry is *witness*. One way of understanding "witness" is as our response to the Truth of God's presence with us. Witness may be a life well lived. It may be conveyed in narrative, in relationship or by example at a distance. It may be helpful on occasion to ask, "How does anyone else who encounters me know about my faith? What about their experience of me is an observable witness to my faith?"

To advance our consideration of models of Christian leadership, let us step together into the Biblical world. After the stressful events of the last supper and crucifixion, some disciples of Jesus are walking on the road, reflecting with one another about the still disconnected pieces of experience they had shared. A stranger joins them and asks what they are talking about. The stranger is the risen Christ! The practice of reflection entered into by these faithful was helped along by the presence of Christ who expanded their understanding. Companionship is a way of leading. We see in this story (Luke 24:13-32), that reflecting in community is helpful. It may even be a place of encounter with Christ the Teacher!

The apostle Paul was on the road to Damascus, continuing his work as a defender of the faith when he was struck with an experience of divine encounter. Paul was a powerful persecutor of the followers of Jesus until something changed his heart. He was, in a manner of speaking, well-prepared and passionate about his perceived calling. His divine encounter had the effect of a wake up call—as though something said, "Hey Paul, good show of enthusiasm and skill, but you're heading the wrong way."

What these stories have in common is the sense of journey, movement, and change. When eyes are open in the process of reflection, new understanding is possible, and new awareness of Christ's presence is also possible.

Even if you don't have a long walk planned, it is possible to live in the sense of a journey by staying in the habit of reflection—seeking to be aware of Christ's presence, and to be willing to have your understanding radically changed as new insights are made available to you. This willingness to be changed by divine encounter means that the perceivable witness to one's faith is necessarily a posture of willingness and expectancy. Other witness and ministry will be apparent in particular situations.

Servant Leadership

One popular model of leadership often touted as the Christian's best model is servant leadership. The phrase "Servant Leadership" was coined by Robert K. Greenleaf in "The Servant as Leader," an essay that he first published in 1970. In that essay, he said:

The servant-leader is servant first… It begins with the natural feeling that one wants to serve, to serve first. Then conscious choice brings one to aspire to lead. That person is sharply different from one who is leader first, perhaps because of the need to assuage an unusual power drive or to acquire material possessions…The leader-first and the servant-first are two extreme types. Between them there are shadings and blends that are part of the infinite variety of human nature.[1]

Reading Scripture and studying the life of Jesus, one can find many examples that reflect the preceding understanding of servant leadership (foot washing, feeding, healing, etc.). Servant leadership as defined above is part of the life modeled by Jesus. In addition to these snapshots of Jesus' leadership style, we can also see that he led and ministered and taught in some other ways. Because much of the contemporary Christian movement is focused on the idea that the most important thing we can learn about the life of Jesus is that he died on the cross, Servant Leadership carries the majority favor. Given what we have examined so far in Scripture and Friends tradition, it seems clear that Quakers will not necessarily be easily persuaded that self-sacrifice and suffering are the only or even best models for leadership.

Robert Barclay was careful to explain his convincement experience as growing out of an exposure to the power of God present with a gathered meeting for worship. In this experience, he felt the goodness in him increase and the sin in him decrease. This divine encounter fed his passion for pursuing the course of his life with a seeker's excitement and passion for continuing and increasing experiences of divine encounter. As we

---

[1] "What is Servant Leadership?" Available from http://www.greenleaf.org/whatissl/index.html; Internet; accessed 11 June 2008.

covered at the very beginning of this study, it was Barclay and his later editor Dean Freiday who emphasized the fact that early Friends were "convinced" of the Gospel Truth and then spent the balance of their lives "converting" so that their lives spoke a living testimony in witness of their divine encounter.

In Luke 10, we can read of the encounter of Jesus with Mary and Martha in their home.

Pause now to read Luke 10:38-42.

Jesus is at the house of Martha who is serving. Mary sits like a sponge at the feet of Jesus, learning. We hear Jesus react to Martha's busyness. This passage has been read with many contexts—to show the contemplative way (Mary's) against and superior to the active path (Martha's), and even to show women as inherently jealous and competitive because these sisters seek Jesus' intervention in their spat. This example is helpful to our consideration of leadership because it illustrates one actively involved in service who has become detached from the Teacher, who is chastised for placing serving above being attentive to the Teacher. The better path is to stay in communication with Christ. Out of the mouth of Jesus we hear, "Serving is not the better choice. Only one thing is important, not all these things that distract you."

In Matthew 14, we see another example of Jesus instructing followers in leadership.

Pause now to read Matthew 14:13-21.

While this story tells of a miracle, a close reading of the dialogue between Jesus and the disciples also shows a leader returning responsibility to his followers. Jesus retreats from the crowds to a boat and then comes ashore to serve (as in servant leadership), but when the disciples ask Jesus to make the crowds go away before it was time to eat, Jesus says no. He tells the disciples not to send the crowds away but to feed them. He helps with problem solving (the loaves and the fishes), and he provides a public role model (prayers of thanks before sharing), but then he gives the disciples the responsibility of feeding the crowds. In this example, we see Jesus saying no to a request to avoid responsibility, but also staying available as a resource and problem-solver. If we read this as a narrative about a teacher teaching, we see that he is encouraging the exhausted and self-doubting disciples to do more than they thought possible.

Pause now to read Galatians 4:19.

Paul uses the image of giving birth to describe his relationship with the Galatians. In fact, he notes that he is in travail again, waiting for Christ to be born in them. Not to be overlooked is that Paul is involved in the birthing of Christ in the faithful, which refers to a kind of continued responsibility for evangelism of the experiential variety. It is not knowledge or creed, but an indwelling presence that wants them prepared to serve him. In this example, we see mothering as a kind of leadership. A mother is one who starts, nurtures but ultimately releases the newborn to its own responsibility. This sense of balancing nurture with the freedom that teaches responsibility is a persistent theme in Scripture and tradition.

In Daniel 1, we read about King Nebuchadnezzar who is outwardly powerful. He captures youth of another tribe and wants them prepared to serve him. We hear about this because Daniel declines the food of the king's table. Pulling out this part of the story, one may observe Nebuchadnezzar's power as dominating and possessive. In addition, he dictates what his followers (involuntary though they may be) are able to eat. In one sense, he offers them the bounty of his table. In another, he requires that they take it (until Daniel rejects it). In this example, we see that leading is directing or influencing the movement of a person or group. *Following* is consciously or unconsciously being susceptible to the leading influence of another.

For Christians, and Quakers in particular, our style of worship indicates an orientation—that we intentionally, consciously and with conviction orient ourselves to be led by Christ. This pursuit is supported by our worship practices, individual and corporate spiritual disciplines, teaching and learning from Scripture, tradition and one another.

Who Leads and (from) Where?

In addition to leading from in front, it's possible to lead from behind. This might be leading like a sheep dog, a teacher, or a recording clerk. There are leaders who do the work for you. There are leaders who do the work without you. And, there are leaders who ask why you're not doing the work.

Jesus washed feet. Jesus upended tables and yelled. Jesus healed. Jesus retreated. Jesus chastised his most faithful followers for being afraid in a storm. We read in Luke 22 that Jesus is among us as one who serves.

> But he said to them, 'The kings of the Gentiles lord it over them; and those in authority over them are called benefactors. [26]But not so with you; rather the greatest among you must become like the youngest, and the leader like one who serves. [27]For who is greater, the one who is at the table or the one who serves? Is it not the one at the table? But I am among you as one who serves.'[2]

It is important not to read just this section to understand how to be a faithful and effective disciple doing leadership in the world. Jesus self-identifies as one who serves. We must feel invited to read the entire narrative of his life and therein to read a wide diversity of activities as service and as leadership.

---

[2] Luke 22: 25-27.

Exercises

Think (or refer) back to verbs for God you identified in an earlier study (Chapter 2), and with the information and consideration that has come to you since, answer these questions:

1. What have you come to understand about the way God leads you?

2. What have you come to understand about the way you are to follow God?

Recall the images of God that your chosen verbs indicate. Let your verbs lead you to images, perhaps nouns or extended metaphors, and then answer the following questions.

1. How is God present in the world?

2. How is God present in the lives of individuals?

3. How is God present in the life of a community?

Universal Ministry Implications

"There are two ways of spreading light: To be the candle or the mirror that reflects it."
—Edith Wharton

"All I know to do is to light the candle that has been given to me."
—Fred Rogers, a.k.a. "Mister Rogers"

Early Friends rejected the model of ministerial leadership held by the Church of England and the Roman Catholic Church from which the Church of England had separated. These denominations assert a hierarchy of ministry that is conveyed from generation to generation of ministerial leaders by outward sacraments, including the laying on of hands that is part of apostolic succession. Apostolic succession is the belief that there is a continuous and unbroken line of priesthood from the apostles chosen by Jesus to the present day leadership of the Roman Catholic Church. The Church of England and its branches also lay claim to apostolic succession, which is an area of disagreement with Roman Catholics. Early Friends stepped aside from all notion of intermediary influence except for that of Christ, whose true Presence is universally available.

So What Is the Good News?

The narratives of the life of Jesus in the Bible are often called "The Gospels." In addition to telling the major events in the life and death of Jesus, these books capture the stories of the people around Jesus, including the disciples. Simon and Andrew were called away from working in the family business; Matthew was chastised for being a tax collector and called away from that work.

In thinking about these calling stories, it may be helpful to frame the question, "When does the shift from student to disciple happen?" Is it the experience of being called or the experience of accepting a call? If it is God calling, is one more or less able to determine a date and time that a call was received for a specific ministry? What about the call to discipleship?

Pause to read Psalm 139.

Friends become convinced of the Truth through a direct encounter with God. The time following a person's convincement encounter contains his or her "conversion," which is the work of bringing one's life into alignment with the teachings of Christ, the Inner Teacher. The Teacher is accessible to all and is known as "That of God" by some contemporary Friends. Christ the Teacher is also known as Christ the Word. In this language, Christ is the expression of God's love and intentions for creation. In addition, Christ is regarded as the second Adam. Since and because of the coming of Christ to Earth, humankind is born with the ability to become that part of creation about which God can say, "It is good." Christ's identity as the New Adam, a popular image among Early Friends, describes the effect of the Incarnation of the Word of God—we see in the New Adam the power of God manifesting, and we begin to learn to live in that power through deepening our relationship with the living Christ.

The historic and continuing testimony of Friends against participation in outward sacraments stems from early Friends' conviction that such outward forms could be empty or distracting from the real transforming effects of Grace happening in a person of faith. As Paul said to the Galatians, Grace is an experience of having Christ born into a person and into a worshipping community.

Exercise

1. Think of a job or volunteer role in which you have had a manager or supervisor. Use the space below to list the characteristics you believe to be signs of a good leader.

   A good leader…

2. As you are able, identify verbs that describe the way a good leader (one that you are willing to follow) behaves.

   A good leader…

In Your Worship Community

1. Consult your yearly meeting book of discipline and search for the word leadership. If you have access to an electronic version, you might enjoy searching the text for "leader," "leadership," "leading," and "led." If you have only a paper version, check the index and table of contents for topics related to leadership to see what is recommended.

2. Obtain a list of all volunteers and committee members in your monthly meeting. Next to each name, identify age, number of years in your meeting, and gender. Use this information as a starting point to identify the "profile" of leadership in your meeting. What tendencies do you notice? What gaps or underused groups do you notice? How does the number of active volunteers measure against the number of volunteer roles in the meeting? How does this number measure against weekly attendance and attendance at business meeting?

CHAPTER SEVEN

Disciple Leadership, A Friends Model

The original message of George Fox, which gathered the Society of Friends, was never systematically formulated by him. It was essentially the faith, based on personal experience, that God and man have direct relationship and mutual correspondence. This was not, in the first instance, a doctrine, but a live and throbbing experience. George Fox kept his faith as concrete as possible and avoided as far as one can, abstract phrases which tend to become mere words. [1]
– Rufus Jones

In previous chapters, through various lenses, we have considered Quaker vocabulary and understandings of God. As Rufus Jones notes in the quotation above, Friends founder George Fox's sense of relationship and correspondence with God was not a doctrine but an experience that he spent his life conveying to others, as if extending an invitation that they too might encounter God this way. Though not concrete in any academic, well-argued sense, Fox's passionate expression of faith was concrete in that it was not comprised of a list of vocabulary terms or theological or doctrinal statements. It has seemed helpful in this exploration of leadership among Friends to emphasize vocabulary as a way of

---

[1] Rufus Jones, "The spiritual message of the Religious Society of Friends," in *World Conference Report of Commission* I (1937): 7-16, cited in New England Yearly Meeting, *Faith and Practice*, 61-62.

identifying what is understood and meant, collectively and individually, about the natures of God and humanity, and about the relationship between God and humanity. It is now time to turn with focus to a Friends model of leadership that we will call Disciple Leadership.

Friends' essential experience of the true presence and persistent availability of Christ as Teacher indicates an equally persistent possibility of *communication with* and *responsiveness to* God. The life of Jesus reveals to us in a unique way the love and intentions of God for the world. This life and our witness of it are together a teaching method in which incarnation is the content and the prescription. Jesus lived fully in response to his communications and relationship with God. By incarnating, Christ who is a lesson from God (God's Word), communicates to us the content of what it means to live a life of faith. In addition, the Biblical witness of the incarnation (life, teachings, ministry, and death of Jesus) offers lessons in what a human can be (Christ is the second Adam and reveals our potential).

The organizing principle in all of this desire to communicate with God and respond faithfully to divine revelation has been named by some Friends "Gospel Order." To understand this term, it may be helpful to consider the meaning of Gospel, which Sandra Cronk ably addresses:

> "Gospel" does not refer primarily to the intellectual content of faith or a religious message. It is the actual life, power, and reality of the relationship with God. Intellectual beliefs only refer to this reality. Faith for Friends was not a matter of accepting certain tenets of belief, although they certainly had such. Faith was

living in the life and power of relationship with
Christ.[2]

Jesus provided an ultimate example of living
faithfully in relationship to God. He sought God's
Presence and leading in the desert and in the garden,
both times of doubt that led to discernment, affirmation
and a sense of divine companionship. All the while, he
responded to what he felt most called to do in the given
moment. The popular phrase, "What Would Jesus Do?"
has tremendous potential to assist one seeking to live as a
leader who is practicing disciple leadership.

To consider offering leadership from a posture that
expects to be led by Christ's Presence, one must also stay
tethered to the community being served and to God's
larger plan for creation. This latter intention may seem
hampered by the fact that God's will and God's
revelation are always partial, at least when perceived
through human reason, which is limited.

Lloyd Lee Wilson defines Gospel Order as follows:

Gospel order is the order established by God that
exists in every part of creation, transcending the
chaos that seems so often prevalent. It is the right
relationship of every part of creation, however small,
to every other part and to the Creator. Gospel order
is the harmony and order which God established at
the moment of creation, and which enables the
individual aspects of creation to achieve that quality
of being which God intended from the start, about
which God could say that "it was very good."

---

[2] Sandra L. Cronk, *Gospel Order: A Quaker Understanding of Faithful
Church Community* (Philadelphia: Pendle Hill, 1991), 5.

Wilson goes on to describe Gospel order as "an organizing principle by which Friends come to a clearer understanding of our relationship to God in all of the divine manifestations and the responsibilities of that relationship."[3] The responsibilities that go with holding up one's end of the relationship with God provide the inspiration, the task, and the compulsion of persons seeking to live faithfully.

In every opportunity for decision-making, available options either primarily reflect a gospel-ordered vision or a worldly vision for that situation. Because community is key to Friends' understanding of how Gospel order is approached and promoted, one seeking to tap into this stream of thought for leadership purposes must remember that the worshipping community is a vital center and anchor.

> ...The basic understanding of Friends... has been that God is present with the faithful community, not with individuals; that it is in the faith community that the divine will is truly known, divine blessings are shared, and Friends are able to build one another up in the faith. A solitary Quaker is an oxymoron.[4]

Questions for Reflection

Take some time to reflect on the following questions based on your response to this chapter's opening thoughts.

---

[3] Wilson, *Essays on the Quaker Vision of Gospel Order*, 3.
[4] Ibid., 20.

1. How is God present in the world? How are you
    present in the world? Where do you meet God in
    the world?

2. How often do you experience a "mutual
    correspondence" with God? How and how often
    do you seek this mutual correspondence? What
    do you "talk" about?

3. In addition to having skills required for a
    particular role, what practices or awareness would
    a person seeking to be a "Disciple Leader" (one
    who follows the living Christ) need to have?

Insights from the Wider World of Friends (and friends)

Friends believed that God would manifest this new
order in the fabric of the social, political, and
economic life of the whole society. Indeed they felt
that ultimately this new order would affect all of
creation, restoring all things to their right
relationship with God and with each other.[5]

Jesus doesn't provide us with an explanation of the
meaning of the parables or add footnotes to bolster
his point. The sayings of Jesus are quite unlike most
lectures that we hear. They are not laid out
didactically like the traditional three point sermon.
To grasp the meaning of Jesus' teachings requires our
participation, and who we are and what we bring

---

[5] Cronk, *Gospel Order*, 5.

with us will have much to do with how we
understand what Jesus has to say to us.[6]

To speak of the kingdom is to speak of Jesus, who
makes the kingdom the center of his message. He is
God, who comes into history and makes of this
particular moment the favorable time for proclaiming
the gift of the kingdom. To accept the gift is to
commit oneself to meet its demands.[7]

The Teacher teaches only everlasting Truth, which is,
in the first instance, about His own nature, as savior,
true shepherd, priest, bishop and prophet—the
"offices" of the messiah. The Teacher will also teach
those who listen how to worship rightly and how to
understand the Scriptures and the parables. He will
show them who their false teachers have been and
will give ways by which they can have assurance that
they are no longer misled. They will know Christ's
voice and thus be able to discern true from false
teaching and teachers.[8]

Questions for reflecting with f/Friends on the
question of discipleship:

1. If we accept that Jesus is the Word of God—the
   living expression of what God would say to
   creation, in creation—how can we engage in
   leadership roles in the world and still live into an

---

[6] Hugh T. Kerr, *The Simple Gospel: Reflections on Christian Faith*
(Louisville: Westminster/John Knox Press, 1991), 16.
[7] Gustavo Gutierrez, *The God of Life* (Maryknoll, NY:Orbis Books, 1991),
67.
[8] Paul A Lacey, *Education and the Inward Teacher*, Pendle Hill Pamphlet
278 (Wallingford, PA: Pendle Hill Publications, 1988), 5.

active discipling role with Christ whom we
acknowledge as this communication?

2. How can we encourage one another, peers and
    younger Friends, to lead from a living, changing,
    unpredictable relationship with God? How can
    we learn to see God's hand in leadings we would
    rather not follow?

3. When seeking to offer "Kingdom of God
    solutions" (manifesting the love of God) in the
    world in areas in which we have leadership
    responsibility or participant responsibility, what
    "handles" are available to us to keep us from ego
    tripping, closing off to the possibility of on-going
    revelation, or simply making decisions that seek
    earthly rewards over the companionship of Christ
    in our work?

Consulting Scripture

In small groups, read each of the passages aloud and
consider the question: *What clue(s) does this passage offer
to being a disciple? And what clues to being a disciple
leader?*

Let the word of Christ dwell in you richly; teach and
admonish one another in all wisdom; and with
gratitude in your hearts sing psalms, hymns, and
spiritual songs to God. [17]And whatever you do, in
word or deed, do everything in the name of the Lord
Jesus, giving thanks to God the Father through him.[9]

---

[9] Colossians 3:16-17.

One of the scribes came near and heard them disputing with one another, and seeing that he answered them well, he asked him, 'Which commandment is the first of all?' [29]Jesus answered, 'The first is, "Hear, O Israel: the Lord our God, the Lord is one; [30]you shall love the Lord your God with all your heart, and with all your soul, and with all your mind, and with all your strength." [31]The second is this, "You shall love your neighbor as yourself." There is no other commandment greater than these.'[10]

Hear, O Israel: The Lord is our God, the Lord alone. [5]You shall love the Lord your God with all your heart, and with all your soul, and with all your might. [6]Keep these words that I am commanding you today in your heart. [7]Recite them to your children and talk about them when you are at home and when you are away, when you lie down and when you rise. [8]Bind them as a sign on your hand, fix them as an emblem on your forehead, [9]and write them on the doorposts of your house and on your gates.[11]

He has told you, O mortal, what is good; and what does the Lord require of you but to do justice, and to love kindness, and to walk humbly with your God?[12]

---

[10] Mark 12:28-31.
[11] Deuteronomy 6:4-9.
[12] Micah 6:8.

Disciple Leadership

It is time to produce a definition or set of characteristics for disciple leadership. Read the following and use the spaces below to add more clarifying details.

To the world, the disciple leader expresses a centeredness, in which her/his life rises out of a deep commitment to a living faith that acknowledges a present God who is active in the world and who encourages participation in the unfolding Kingdom by persons of faith. A disciple leader is one who is seeking to bring about God's intention for some area of creation in which the leader has influence.

A disciple leader acknowledges the following:

- That there is a difference between being skilled and being called, although these areas overlap at times.
- That some callings are for a period of time and others are for a lifetime.
- That God's intention for the world may be partially revealed at any time.
- That a person of faith must cultivate and practice searching out the Presence of God. This may include looking for clues, identifying "verbs for God," and being willing to be changed by any encounter.
- That God calls humans into communities.
- That worshipping communities are called to be incarnations of Christ on earth.

- That Jesus was not simply a suffering servant, but also a man who used many methods and was called to many actions.
- That Scripture and tradition show a variety of roles and possibilities for leaders.
- That leadership requires followership.
- That discipleship is not a job, a skill set, or a set of beliefs. It is an orientation, a foundation, a habituation from which all of one's life is lived.

Add more characteristics of disciple leaders.

_____

_____

_____

In Your Worship Community

- How do the experiences of First Day (worship, praise, teaching, learning, sharing fellowship, etc.) reflect each participant's relationship with God?

- How do the other six days of the week reflect the experience of First Day?

- In what area(s) of your life (in or outside of meeting) are you able to practice being a disciple leader?

CHAPTER EIGHT

The Meeting as Spiritual
Community and Anchor

The participatory nature of Friends worship is often a point of attraction for seekers. The ideas of universal ministry and the availability of the Presence of Christ indicate the important theological emphasis Friends hold on the work of the Spirit and on continuing revelation. Unlike some of our siblings in the Church, we place Scripture and tradition behind the experience of Christ. We consider them important interpretative aids, but accessories to the experience of the living Christ. Friends approach worship with a sense of expectancy that clearly means that they are gathered together, willing to be changed and informed by God, who is actively among us.

In his book, *Silence and Witness*, Michael Birkel explains early Friends' sense of divine encounter this way:

Early Friends' experience of the Inward Light was not as a cosy fire but rather a relentless search beam that showed them their sinfulness. The Light at first exposed their capacity for evil but then led to the victory of good over evil within them. A sense of inward peace followed—often after a lengthy internal conflict—and a deep sense of community with other

Friends who had been through the same harrowing experience.[1]

With these weighty understandings at the root of our faith and practice, there is no wonder that the role of the meeting community as anchor is key to a worshipping community's vitality. Friends come together because there are simply things that happen in relationship to God and to one another that could not happen without community participation.

There is a dual focus to Friends faith and practice that requires attention to the inner life and compels action in the outer world. Without an anchor to hold one accountable to the tradition and the community, an individual would be more able to lose sight of the presence, intimations, shadow and echo of God's presence.

As Howard Brinton notes:

> …Quakerism, though primarily directed toward the inner life, accepts objective historical events. Chief among them is the central event in the history of Christianity, the revelation of God in human terms through Jesus of Nazareth. If God had not revealed himself both outwardly in history and inwardly in experience, the outward revelation would have lacked power and meaning and the inward revelation would remain formless and vague. Only as the outward eye of time and the inward eye of eternity are focused on

[1] Birkel, *Silence and Witness,* 22.

a single fact does that fact attain the three-dimensional quality of Truth." [2]

God did reveal Godself inwardly and outwardly, and so we are an expectant community living in the confidence that a three-dimensional Truth is imaginable, and perhaps available.

The Body of Christ

Roman Catholic theologian Avery Dulles writes that if we use the image of the "Body of Christ" to describe a worshipping community as Paul does in Romans 12 and in 1 Corinthians 12, "the main point is the mutual union, mutual concern, and mutual dependences of the members of the local community upon one another."[3] Dulles also points out that as the Body of Christ, the church body has "an inbuilt vital principle [the Holy Spirit] thanks to which it can grow, repair itself, and adapt itself to changing needs."

The two fundamental places to note Friends worshipping communities functioning as bodies of Christ (or member groups of a larger single body of Christ) are in meeting for worship and in meeting for worship with a concern for business.

Howard Brinton writes that the Religious Society of Friends holds a doctrine that was central to the early Christian movement—the belief that the Spirit, which unites members of the prepared congregation, is poured out on the congregation ready to receive it. "This

---

[2]Howard Brinton, *Friends for 300 Years* (1952), xii and xiv, cited in of New England Yearly Meeting, *Faith and Practice*.
[3] Avery Dulles, *Models of the Church*, 50.

Spirit... unites all the members into a single organic whole, the body of Christ. The individual experience of inward oneness with an invisible Reality is also an experience of the mystical union of individuals with one another."

Take time to consider the following questions before moving on to the consideration of Meeting for Worship and Meeting for Worship with a Concern for Business.

1. What is your initial reaction to the use of the term "body of Christ?" What definition of it comes to mind on first thought?

2. Does your meeting use this term to describe itself or to describe any larger group of persons of faith?

3. What relationship do you imagine between the presence of God (known and experienced as Light, Inward Teacher, Living Christ, etc.) and the community you worship with? Is your community formed or living in response to a sense of the Living Presence?

Meeting for Worship

In the excitement of their discovery that Christ was alive and had "come to teach His people Himself," early Friends gathered for worship fully expecting the Spirit to be present, and out of their hushed expectancy they entered into a fellowship with God that changed their lives. In the course of such worship came new revelations of Truth and a force that drove Friends out into the world to spread the news and to serve humanity.[4]

As in meeting for worship, the silence is an opportunity to open oneself to the guiding hands of the Holy Spirit. It is not a time to organize one's thoughts to devise the strategy of an argument to persuade others. ... That quiet encounter with God can renew my faith in the collective wisdom of the community, when it is also grounded in God. Finding God's love in the silence awakens love for others in the room, and the community is ready to be led.[5]

In addition to weekly meeting for worship, there is Meeting for Worship with a Concern for Business, which is usually a monthly occasion in the local worshipping community. The business meeting is the occasion when the gathered body turns from expectant worship to a combination of expectant worship and business. The business may include aspects of corporate discernment about mission and outreach or about finances and committee structure. It is literally the place of caretaking daily tasks in the life of the meeting. Three paradoxes indicate why business meetings are a point of vitality in meetings: 1. the life and death of Jesus, 2. the understanding of a Kingdom ordered by Godly principles with another ordered by worldly principles, and 3. the idea that Friends must respond to an

---

[4] New England Yearly Meeting, *Faith and Practice*, 95.
[5] Birkel, *Silence and Witness*, 69.

individual call to become part of a group that must respond to a corporate call. Business meeting is the place where corporate spiritual practices allow a group to move faithfully and united toward a purpose seeded and directed by God.

As one example of how this is conceived, Ann Arbor Friends Meeting states clearly on their website a definition of the business meeting as "the central means for making decisions, translating concerns into action, and considering matters relating to the organization of the Meeting and its program and activities as an ongoing religious group." Indicating their certainty that the group is called to act as one body, they further note:

> Friends assume that in the transaction of business the Meeting will be able to act in unity. If unity cannot be achieved, the Meeting defers action. Friends do not reach decisions by voting, since we believe that voting may be a method of imposing the will of the majority on the minority; it may serve to divide rather than to unify a group. Instead of voting, the Meeting reaches decisions by "sense of the Meeting," by which is meant the Meeting's sense of God's will. [6]

The explanation of "sense of the meeting" includes an important theological foundation: the meeting functions as a unit, and God is presumed to have an intention ("will") for the meeting as a unit to follow.

[6]"What is Meeting for Worship in Business?" Available from *http://www.annarborfriends.org/worshipforbusiness.shtml;* Internet; (accessed 22 June 2008).

North Pacific Yearly Meeting similarly holds:

Friends conduct business together in the faith that
there is one divine Spirit which is accessible to all
persons; when Friends wait upon, heed and follow
the Light of Truth within them, its Spirit will lead to
unity. This faith is the foundation for any group
decision...it is of prime importance that Friends
understand and follow this procedure for business in
the Monthly Meeting...[This] principle underlies all
activities of the Society of Friends.[7]

Wilmington Yearly Meeting and North Carolina
Yearly Meeting (FUM) both include versions of the
following in their Faith and Practice:

Waiting for Guidance
The practice of holding meetings for business
following a period of worship opens the way for a
continuation of the religious fellowship experienced
during such a period. The same reverent waiting that
operates in the meetings for worship is also helpful in
seeking divine guidance and unity of action in the
transaction of business. The right conduct of these
meetings even in routine matters is important to the
spiritual life of all. Such meetings are a part of the
organized undertaking to promote the Kingdom of

---

[7] North Pacific Yearly Meeting, "Friends' Method of Reaching Decisions,"
North Pacific Yearly Meeting of the Religious Society of Friends
(Quakers) *Faith and Practice*, (n.d.), chap. 8, available from
http://www.npym.org/fnp/main.html; Internet; (accessed 22 June 2008).

God. Service in them may be rightfully regarded as service for Him.

Friendly Method

It is the practice of Friends to give unhurried and sympathetic consideration to all proposals and expressions of opinion. They endeavor to respect an earnest and sincere minority and, if it seems necessary, may postpone action until they have secured more light on the question at issue and have attained a greater degree of unanimity. Each Friend should be certain that the expressed concern and comments are led by the Spirit of God. After due consideration has been given to all points of view, it is the duty of the clerk of the Meeting to weigh carefully the various expressions and to state what is believed to be the will of the meeting.[8]

And, New York Yearly Meeting describes Meeting for Worship with a concern for business with a similar explanation of the God's availability:

We look with tender hearts, especially during meetings for worship with a concern for business, for one another's spiritual vision. Truths of the Spirit may come from any of us. ...Our belief that people can continually discover more about the will of God makes us eschew dogma. We search for ways to meet human need in shared worship and open ourselves to disagreement as a path to God's higher truths. The Spirit leads our community to creative action, occasionally in ways that transcend reason, as we

---

[8] North Carolina Yearly Meeting (FUM), *Faith and Practice* (2004), pp. 59-60.

listen for God's voice in our prayers and in the messages we have for each other. [9]

Expectancy in worship means:

We are gathered together...
We are willing to be changed...
We are informed by God...
God is actively among us.

Exercise

Take a few moments to reflect on these questions about your own experience of meeting for worship and meeting for worship with a concern for business.

1. How do you prepare for meeting for worship? When and with what consistency does this preparation occur? Do you expect that others in your community prepare similarly?

2. In what ways is your worshipping community an anchor for you? In other words, what other aspects of your life are held in place, or rooted, because of your involvement with your meeting?

3. When looking at the definition of "expectant worship" presented here, which of the following feel most true in your meeting? Which seem to be areas that need improvement? [We are gathered together, willing to be changed and informed by God who is actively working among us.]

---

[9] New York Yearly Meeting, *Book of Discipline* (2001), p.26.

4. How well is your meeting's meeting for worship with an attention to business attended? Does the quality and quantity of participation support the idea that your meeting is a united body, called together for a purpose?

Corporate Spiritual Practice

Discipleship occurs in a specific context, and leadership also begins and manifests in a particular context. A person with gifts, skills, or a particular call to leadership will rise to this ministry out of a community where s/he has been involved.

Communities that keep good soil turned for naming and nurturing gifts for leadership and other ministry areas tend to be communities that acknowledge the inner and outer elements of the spiritual life, and also engage together in a covenantal experience of spiritual practice with a group.

Some basic characteristics of communities that have a corporate spiritual identity include:

- Members show up even when they don't want to, and participate faithfully and expectantly.
- Members extend their desires to include the spiritual well-being of others and not just themselves.

- Members know and teach others that the full participation of every individual in the community makes the community fuller, more well-rounded, and more available to do God's work with a diversity of gifts.

Are there others that you would add?

_____

_____

_____

Exercise

Call to mind your community and the way you came to be part of it. Imagine that God blesses your participation with this particular community, and see whether you can imagine what you bring that is uniquely yours that is of benefit to the community. What role do you play in the body that is comprised of your fellow worshippers?

_____

_____

_____

Growing Edges

In sustainable agriculture, some of the most fertile areas are the places of intersection and of difference. At the edge of a field, where the forest just begins with a few trees that mingle with the grass field, there is great opportunity for a diversity of species to flourish. Plants and animals that require synergistic relationship, thrive on difference and distinction and create feedback loops that improve life for the entire system.

In faith communities, this condition of thriving among a diversity of gifts, interests and inclinations, may also be true but the common ground of the community and the commitment to being part of the community is what allows difference to be productive. In addition to the common ground established by Meeting for Worship and Meeting for Worship with a Concern for Business, communities may choose to engage in group spiritual practices. Such practices might include:

- Bible study
- Topically specific conversation groups (for example, the peace testimony, Friends and money, Friends education, Quaker history, etc.)
- Healing prayer meetings
- Structured times to pray with Scripture as in praying the Psalms
- Clearness committees

In the next chapter, we will consider the ways in which the meeting is involved in activities that make it both a spiritual community and a social community. To insure that the spiritual life of the meeting flourishes, it is important to identify some corporate practices that are specifically focused on spiritual nurture of the individual members and of the body they comprise. While potlucks and social activism certainly can feed the individual and corporate spiritual life of Friends, study, prayer, and practical discernment may provide a sharper focus on cultivating the inward life.

Exercise

Take some time with the following questions.

1. In what activities have you participated in your current worship community or in some previous community that most strongly fed the group's spiritual life and connection to God?

_____

_____

_____

2. Consult your yearly meeting's book of discipline or faith and practice to see what advices or queries are offered on cultivating the corporate body as a spiritual body. How does your lived experience measure against what is recommended?

_____

_____

_____

This has been a chapter about taking the idea of body of Christ from something of dogma or intellectual understanding to a living and acting manifestation of Christ in the world. By giving attention to the constitution of the particular body we belong to, we can begin to see what gifts we uniquely bring. By looking at the quality of participation in meeting for worship and business meeting, we can begin to understand the metaphor of being a body of Christ or part of a larger body of Christ (the incarnated lives of the faithful, in groups, living their testimony to the Truth out in the world.)

Leadership happens in context. In the context of good ground, gifts are sought, named, nurtured, mentored, and put to work as part of a united body working for the purposes of God on earth. In the context of good ground, Friends can identify and stay close to the root, which is the presence of God with us, best apprehended in the posture of expectancy. From this context, we may begin to see clearly what opportunities for conceiving and maintaining a disciple leadership style are actually possible within any given monthly meeting and for members who seek to experience the worshipping community as an anchor that sustains them as they lead and minister elsewhere in the world.

In Your Worship Community

Sit with others in your meeting, perhaps in groups of 3 or 4, and consider the following:

1. How many leaders do we currently have in our meeting?

2. How did they come to lead?

3. How did they come to make it on the list we are generating in this discussion? (Is it by role or by perceived authority that we know them?)

4. Is our meeting good ground for growing leaders—do we function as a united body, seeking to minister in response to the Truth as we have collectively apprehended and discerned it?

5. For members who offer more of their giftedness to other work in the world, in what ways does this community provide an anchor?

CHAPTER NINE

Theological Reflection on/and the Life of the Meeting

Together with Jesus, the disciples constituted a contrast society, symbolically representing the new and renewed Israel. ... The community of the disciples, with its exceptional style of life, was intended to attract attention, like a city set upon a mountaintop or lantern in a dark place. It had a mission to remind the rest of the people of the transcendent value of the Kingdom of God, to which the disciples bore witness. It was therefore important for them to adopt a manner of life that would make no sense apart from their intense personal faith in God's providence and his fidelity to his promises.[1]

Given Friends' strong foundation in the earliest Friends' desire to return to a model of church akin to that of first century Christians, it seems Friends would easily and naturally embrace a model of leadership that is after the pattern of the first disciples. We can see that for early Friends and contemporary Friends, the primary call is to stay close to the guiding presence of God with us. The posture of expectancy Friends take in worship and in living close to the leadings of the Spirit indicates a solid foundation in the belief that God is available and interactive. As discussed in previous chapters, Friends also believe that the in-breaking of God may require

---

[1] Avery Dulles, *Models of the Church*, 209.

something of them. It is the arrangement of Friends in monthly and yearly meetings that gives anchor and structure to what could otherwise deteriorate into self-directed ideas that leave one isolated and unreflected and unmeasured by any community's guidance, tradition, practices and encouragement. Simply, Quaker leaders must rise from the good ground of vital meetings, and they must participate with meetings that are fully functioning bodies of Christ in order to stay close to the sound and appearance of God and God's desires for the world. Meetings and their practices provide the spiritual anchor for leaders, whether they serve in the meeting or in the world.

This chapter, building on the previous two chapters, will be a starting point for meetings to assemble their collective gifts and look for the call embedded in this collection. Important questions will include: *What is God calling this group to in this time? Who are the leaders and the leaders-to-be, and how can they be nurtured in their work? How can others follow with their gifts?*

As this year of study concludes, this final chapter is structured to guide participants through a meeting-of-the-whole retreat. Depending on the percentage of meeting members who attend, these exercises may lend themselves to being a visioning retreat, or a community-building retreat, depending on what is most needed. It is suggested that meetings appoint one or more note-takers to record the outcomes of all exercises and group reflections on these exercises. It is hoped that by entering prayerfully and intentionally into the posture of corporate worship and sustaining this attitude throughout the retreat will facilitate increased awareness of God's presence with and direction for this meeting.

This retreat can be helpfully punctuated with intentional times of prayer, Scripture reading and worship sharing. Please allow significant time for corporate spiritual practices, for it is in worshipping as one body that you will be able to discern and carry on matters of business as one body.

Individual Preparation

> If I try to be or do something noble that has nothing to do with who I am, I may look good to others and to myself for a while. But the fact that I am exceeding my limits will eventually have consequences. I will distort myself, the other, and our relationship---and may end up doing more damage than if I had never set out to do this particular good. When I try to do something that is not in my nature or the nature of the relationship, way will close behind me.... When the gift I give to the other is integral to my own nature, when it comes from a place of organic reality within me, it will renew itself---and me---even as I give it away.[2]
>
>   -- Parker Palmer, *Let Your Life Speak*

Have all retreat participants begin the day with the following questions, knowing that their answers need not be shared, but would be most useful if honest.

1. What is the current state of my relationship to the meeting and to the majority of persons I see in this room today?

---

[2] Parker J. Palmer, *Let Your Life Speak: Listening for the Voice of Vocation.* (San Francisco: Jossey-Bass, 2000), 47.

2. Am I willing to grow and possibly to change, with these Friends as my fellows and my challengers?

3. What limits am I already aware of going into the day's activities?

Corporate Foundations

Use the space below to list the activities, with an emphasis on verbs, that the worshipping community does that fit either as elements of Spiritual Community-building and maintenance or as Social Community-building and maintenance. A few samples are provided one the next page for your encouragement. If there seem to be many that fit in both categories, work together to decide which category is most suitable.

You might complete the sentence: "_____ adds significantly to this meeting's spiritual life/ social life." (choose one)

_____

_____

_____

_____

_____

_____

Social community (verbs and activities)	Spiritual community (verbs and activities)
• Monthly potluck (eating) • Book discussion group (reading) •	• Weekly meeting for worship (worship) • Monthly worship sharing in response to queries (personal theological reflection) •

Looking back at the list you generated, consult with others in the session to see where you have similar and distinct impressions of the spiritual and social nurture the meeting creates and offers. Note that the differences of opinion may relate to the vantage point—the length of time one has been involved, the age of the person, etc. Where differences are noted, go a step further to determine why there are different perceptions.

The Culture of Immediacy

"Staying close to the Guide" may be a less familiar concept than noting that one may "outrun the Guide." It is possible that a monthly meeting or other corporate body may outrun the Guide. However, if everyone in the room is part of the corporate body, there is no clear witness to note when the group has lost sight of its practice or its purpose. For this reason, the gifts of tradition, books of faith and practice, Scripture, and larger/other bodies of Friends to consult with or simply worship with, as a way to remind ourselves to stay attentive to the share of revealed Truth that has been given to us may be helpful. Corporate spiritual practices, including and in addition to weekly worship, help build the meeting's corporate sense of self, and also help build the sturdiness of the anchor that a meeting can be for a leader or any minister.

As has been mentioned in previous chapters, there is a synergistic relationship between the devotional life of the individual and that of the community. These two are the source of the active ministry of the individual and the group. As Patricia Loring notes,

> …personal practice, corporate practice and ethics are inseparable within Quaker formation and transformation. Neither the inner life nor meeting life nor an active relationship with the rest of the world is optional. Prayer that does not issue in deeds of love becomes a form of narcissism or an aesthetic exercise. Activity that does not take time to find its source and grounding in prayer, worship and divine leading becomes dry, exhausting, and exasperating— or an exercise in power.[3]

---

[3] Patricia Loring, *Listening Spirituality, Volume I Personal Spiritual Practices Among Friends* (Washington, D.C. :Openings Press, 1997), 1.

Loring writes that participation in one's own inner cultivation feeds and is fed by corporate worship. Together these two feed the outward expression of faith and vocation in the world. This is our witness in and to the world. The corporate witness of a Friends worshipping community is an outgrowth of the individual and corporate leadings experienced by a particular people in a particular time. Let us now turn our attention to the identity and leadings of the meeting.

Meeting One Another Deeply

In small groups or as a group of the whole, consider each one of the following questions separately. A minimum of 30 minutes is suggested for each question, with time in between to re-gather as a group of the whole to share broad statements about the findings. Note: Time for writing and re-writing allows time for editing. Knowing one another deeply requires a willingness to see and be seen, without too much self-editing.

1. Share names/images used for God in personal and public prayer.

2. Tell about how you kindle the fire of your inner life, your devotional time, or time for connecting with the holy.

3. As a worship sharing exercise, have participants share about a time when they have experienced a significant sense of spiritual community (from any time and place in life), and about their reaction to this sense of spiritual community.

Pause to notice how the gathered group is moving as a body in this moment of this day.

Have participants share with one other person about the experience of completing the Survey of the Body in Chapter Five. Here are some guiding questions:

1. What are your hopes and prayers for this meeting as a meeting?

2. How do these reflect the statements shared earlier about most noteworthy experiences of spiritual community?

3. What gifts and interests do you bring to the meeting from the Survey of the Body exercise? (It may be helpful to capture these in writing on a flipchart or white board for the group to see. Additionally, it may be worth noting which gifts and interests indicate a growing edge for the group or the individual.)

Re-gather as group of the whole, considering all the insights generated and captured from the preceding exercises, and then pose the guiding questions:

What is God calling this group to in this time? Who are the leaders and the leaders-to-be, and how can they be nurtured in their work? How can others follow with their gifts?

From the gifts identified, and the strengths of our meeting as both a social community and a spiritual

*community, what do these gifts indicate about the role
this meeting may play in bringing Kingdom solutions to
the world's problems?*

The Question of Discipleship

Pause to have participants consult the gospel
narratives of the sending out of disciples. (Matthew 10:1-
15, Luke 10:1-12, and Mark 6:7-13). Allow some time
for shared reflection on these passages.

Then reflect on the following:

1. What modifications would this community make
   based on what has been discussed today? In other
   words, as we send leaders and other ministers out
   into the world, or to the front of our meetings,
   what guidance do we offer?

2. What is our covenant with these ministers, and
   what is our agreement with God as we function as
   a body of Christ? How are these two covenants
   related?

Lead on, Lead from, Lead with, and Follow

One respondent to Earlham School of Religion's
1998 consultation with Friends about Quakers in the
U.S. explained that there are calls for a season and calls
for a lifetime vocation. He writes:

[Joseph Rost] says leadership is an influence
relationship among leaders and followers who intend

real changes that reflect their mutual purposes. When you add in the dynamic of the Spirit as being part of that influence relationship, that is a good understanding of leadership among Quakers at their best. To me, this eliminates the situation in which this person is always the leader because of his or her role. That's not what we believe, but we also need this freedom to say this is the time for this person to lead. Let him or her lead. And it is our time to follow.[4]

Pause to consider...

1. When is it your time to follow? To lead? What tools of discernment do you or have you used to know the difference? Does your worship community have tools to assist with these questions?

2. Pause to consult the book of discipline to see what from that resource can serve as a partial answer to the previous question.

One of the amazing graces found in the Quaker sense of being called, prepared, and directed by God for God's work is that the bodies incarnating Christ's love in the world are changing groups. The membership changes, and the ways in which these particular persons of faith are invited to live lives that witness to the Truth that has been given them is unique and timely. Just as the incarnation of Jesus entered time in a particular time for

---

[4] *Among Friends: a consultation with Friends about the condition of Quakers in the U.S. today* (Richmond, Indiana: Earlham Press), 132.

particular purposes, so are we called into meetings for particular purposes.

In Your Worship Community

End this time together in worship, with gratitude and joy for the intentional steps taken to attend to your worship community.

CONCLUSION

Welcome to the Beginning, Again

Now that the study is over, you and your worship community are ready to move faithfully toward what God is calling you to. As we began with the story of entering the church by the front door only to find ourselves at the back of the worship room, we are at the end of the book, but at a new beginning of the story of your faithful witness of your faith. We are also at a new beginning with God as you experience and respond with your daily lives, as individuals and as members of the incarnated body.

Remember the value of good ground for seeds, and do what you can to tend the ground of your meeting and your daily walk with God. Disciple leadership in the manner of Friends requires staying close to the practice of discernment and listening for the voice of God, with a strong and faithful community to help you reflect on the ways God is leading and urging your response.

I close with hope for the continuation of a life lived in faithful witness. Jesus referred to the way to live faithfully when he was asked to name the greatest commandment. He said there are two greatest commandments, to love God and to love your neighbor as yourself. The way to love God that Jesus refers to is stated more fully in Deuteronomy.

Hear, O Israel: The Lord is our God, the Lord alone. [5]You shall love the Lord your God with all your heart, and with all your soul, and with all your might. [6]Keep these words that I am commanding you today in your heart. [7]Recite them to your children and talk about them when you are at home and when you are away, when you lie down and when you rise. [8]Bind them as a sign on your hand, fix them as an emblem on your forehead, [9]and write them on the doorposts of your house and on your gates.[1]

May it be so with you, that you love God with all that you are, from waking to sleeping, in all that you have and do, and that this love and God's Love, pouring through your life and the life of your worship community, will be unmistakable to all who encounter you.

---

[1]Deuteronomy 6:4-9.

Appendix A

Sample Covenant Agreement

This is a sample of a covenant agreement your worship community might use as a guide in writing one that fits the level and components of accountability that would be most helpful.

A COVENANT OF MEETING PARTICIPATION

We the members of _____, in response to the presence and teachings of Christ, believe that God calls us to be a community that willingly leads and is led, in accord with discerned leadings of the Holy Spirit. We affirm our desire to explore and implement a Friends Leadership model that responds to God's invitation to be faithful stewards of the gifts we receive as individuals and as a meeting. To this end, we commit ourselves to faithful participation in this program. We will engage reflectively and actively on the topic of leadership development, and will join with others to promote leadership development in our monthly and yearly meetings and in the wider bodies of the Religious Society of Friends and the Christian movement.

With gratitude, we affirm and support the following persons in their leadings to accept primary responsibility for our meeting's participation in this leadership development program.

1.

2.

3.

4.

Responsibilities of the meeting:
- o Form an ad hoc committee of four participants to anchor this program in the meeting.
- o Offer prayer support to the Friends who step forward as named representatives.
- o Participate in monthly activities related to leadership development.
- o Be open to naming and nurturing gifts for leadership as they are noted in the meeting.
- o Embody a willingness to be transformed.

Responsibilities of individuals on ad hoc committee:
- o Be advocates and contact persons within the meeting for the leadership engagement program.
- o Coordinate and lead monthly events within the meeting to explore leadership
- o Participate in and encourage others to participate in additional events related to themes of leadership development, spiritual formation and other topics generally related to this study. Such additional leadership exploration learning opportunities could involve members of multiple worship communities gathering to learn and reflect together.

We are fully committed to participate in this study, seeking to rediscover and advance a Friends model of leadership development for the betterment of our monthly meeting, the yearly meeting, the Religious Society of Friends and the wider world.

For the ad hoc committee:

_____ Signature: _____
(date)
_____ Signature: _____
(date)
_____ Signature: _____
(date)
_____ Signature: _____
(date)

For the meeting clerk or pastor:

_____ Signature: _____
(date)

Appendix B

Sample Timeline for One-Year Study

This is a suggested timeline for using this book.

Note: The first full-congregation lesson is indicated with an asterisk in the time column.

4-6 months prior to start of program	First readers, consider queries of readiness for individual, community and pastoral involvement. Determine if God is leading you to be a facilitator of this work in your meeting.
3-4 months prior to start of program	Meet with ministry and oversight, the adult religious education committee, or another group to explore greater community interest in undertaking this study.
2-3 months prior to start of program	Facilitating team begins intense engagement with materials on a once-weekly basis, which will take two months.
2 months prior to start of program	Write a covenant agreement that facilitators and others in meeting will sign to solidify commitment to the process.

2 months prior to start of program	Bring conversation to a fuller part of the worship community, either in business meeting or adult religious education forum; include presentations by facilitators who have experienced together some part of the work in the book.
1 month prior to start of program	Plan a portion of business meeting or adult religious education forum to consider queries of readiness for individual, community and pastoral involvement. Revisit covenant agreement and modify as appropriate.
*	First full congregation study of chapter one, which may be broken up over several weeks.
Month 2 of study	Chapter 2
Month 3 of study	Chapter 3
Months 4-5	Chapter 4, continuing into month 5 for survey of meeting gifts and needs and individual gifts and callings
Month 6	Chapter 5
Month 7	Chapter 6
Month 8	Chapter 7

Month 9 or 10   Depending on whether holiday and other vacation breaks have slowed your progress through the material, plan to use Chapters 8 and 9 to guide a full day or day and a half retreat. If an annual planning and fellowship retreat is part of your meeting, this may be a suitable program.

Month 10 or 11   Plan at least one session after the conclusion of Chapter 9 and the retreat to check in on ideas generated and work on plans for implementation. Establish new initiatives and plans for the coming year.

Appendix C

Queries for Readiness to Undertake This Study

The following are intended to give respondents a guided opportunity to consider some of the topics covered in this year of study. While no answer will provide a clear "yes" to participation, it might be helpful to notice the quality of your response to the questions. Are you energized or provoked? Do these considerations bring you to a place of deepening spiritual presence? If so, the material in this study may be fruitful for you at this time. It may be particularly helpful to use these queries in small groups so that your community can reflect on how the group is being affected by the possibility of undertaking this work together.

For the Whole Meeting

In what ways does our worshipping community provide an anchoring presence in my life? In what ways do I serve as part of this anchoring presence for others in my community?

Am I able to commit to faithful participation in a year-long study that may at times be uncomfortable and provocative? What would be helpful to hold me accountable to this commitment?

For Congregational Leadership

Am I willing and able to support an intense, transformative, unpredictable program of study that may change my meeting?

How am I regarded in relationship to other leaders in the meeting, and how am I engaged with the ministries of others in meeting?

What is my role in naming and nurturing gifts, and in what ways have I been free to do this work? In what ways have I felt limited in my ability to do this? What are the sources of limitation?

For Volunteers Who May Feel Led to be Part of the Facilitating Team

How do I understand leadership, and what is my relationship to it?

In what ways am I being called to address leadership needs in my meeting and in the wider world?

What are my most persistent hopes for my worshipping community? What am I doing to make these hopes come true?

Appendix D

Alternative Uses for the Material

This book has been carefully put together for use as a complete program. The material is best used in the order it is presented because there is a cumulative, building effect of studying in this way. Of course, there are ways to use the material productively in smaller pieces for other purposes. Here are some ideas:

- Take a single vocabulary exercise as a stand-alone adult education opportunity. See Chapter One for vocabulary of faith or Chapter Four for terms related to corporate spirituality.

- Use the survey of gifts for individuals in Chapter Four as part of your congregation's annual stewardship drive as a way to reinforce that participation is as important as financial support.

- Alternately, or successively, use the corporate needs exercises in Chapter Four to bring the worshipping group to a clearer articulation of what needs are perceived.

- Use the "Consulting Scripture" exercises in any chapter as a way to open Scripture up to the needs of the community. Read under the same Spirit that inspired its writing.

- Use the "Insights from the Wider World of Friends" section in any chapter to learn about the

ways in which your community has received or
interpreted Friends' practices similarly or
differently than other Friends groups. In
particular, notice what appeals to you and your
community from any new as a result of any new
understandings you may have had.

- Use the closing exercises from each chapter, "In
  Your Worship Community" as queries for
  worship sharing.

- After reading the book, notice which exercises
  hold the most energy for you—both the most and
  least appealing exercises—and bring those to a
  group in your community to do as a shared
  spiritual practice.

Printed in the United States
204163BV00002B/553-660/P